A Great Day School in London

*'A Great Day School in London': the description used by F. W. Walker,
High Master of St Paul's School, in 1866 when he applied unsuccessfully
for the headmastership of KCS.*

A Great Day School in London

A History of King's College School

Thomas Hinde

JAMES
X
JAMES

ISBN 0 907383 610
© King's College School 1995
First published 1995

Printed and bound by Foister & Jagg 1994 Limited

Designed by Bob Speel

New photography by John Spragg

Published by James & James (Publishers) Ltd
Gordon House Business Centre
6 Lissenden Gardens
London NW5 1LX

Half-title page: *Boys in the KCS playing fields, 1899.*
Frontispiece: *Etching of the Great Hall by Sidney Ferris, 1925.*
Opposite Contents page: *The Great Hall as it appeared in 1899, drawn by Henry William Brewer.*

FOREWORD

We are delighted at KCS to have had the opportunity of reviewing the School's historic achievements so close to the centenary of its removal to Wimbledon in 1897. The last Old Boy who was taught in The Strand died recently but King's continues to have great attachment to that period in its history. The illustrations in this book make abundantly clear what an interesting period it was. I am equally pleased that, in the closing years of this century, it will now be possible to assess the astonishing progress of KCS on its Wimbledon site.

Robin Reeve

ROBIN REEVE
SPRING 1995

CONTENTS

CHAPTER ONE

Major – The Council's Man

1831–1866

The decision to found King's College, London, was taken by a great inaugural meeting at the Freemasons' Hall, Westminster, on 21 June 1828. Over that meeting presided the Prime Minister, the Duke of Wellington. More significantly, alongside him on the platform sat no fewer than three archbishops and seven bishops, while the hall was largely filled with other clergymen, for the new college was to be the Church of England's answer to the nonsectarian University College, founded two years earlier. It was the support of the Church of England, religion of the State, which was to gain for King's College a Royal Charter.

The original idea for the new college came from Dr George D'Oyly, Rector of Lambeth, one of the most influential churchmen of the time; while at Lambeth he established no fewer than 13 new churches for its expanding population. Since 1813 he had been chaplain to the Archbishop of Canterbury. When he died in 1846 the College Council acknowledged that 'the design of the Institution was originally conceived by him, and … he was virtually the Founder of the College'. Four months before the inaugural meeting D'Oyly had written an open letter to Robert Peel, Home Secretary, in which he deplored the fact that University College had omitted 'everything connected with Christianity' from its courses, and proposed the founding of a second university in London in which 'an essential part of the education imputed [would] imbue the minds of youth with the principles of Christianity'.

During the following four months it was probably D'Oyly who played the leading part in settling many details of the proposed college, with the result that the Duke was able to present the meeting with resolutions describing its curriculum, government, and financing. All of these the meeting approved. It also resolved that the College was 'to be divided into two departments – a higher department for the elder [students] and a lower department for the younger'. It

Opposite page: *Dr John Richardson Major, the first Head Master.*

was this lower department which became King's College School, and which, conceived as a tail appended to the College to provide it with a flow of students, soon began financially to wag the dog to which it was attached.

Finally, the inaugural meeting appointed a committee of 27 to bring to birth the College it had conceived. By the end of the year this Provisional Committee had defined more closely the College's lower department. It was to be 'totally distinct from the Higher', and would 'consist of a School for the reception of day-scholars'. It would 'be placed under the separate management of a Headmaster appointed by the Council, and a competent number of Under Masters, appointed by him, all members of the Church of England'.

To finance the new College (and School) the Duke asked for £100,000 in the form of donations or the purchase of £100 shares, and said that no work would begin until the full sum was raised. So far so good: the Archbishop of Canterbury headed the list of donors with a gift of £1,000 and by 19 August 1828 £102,000 had been raised or promised. But two difficulties soon arose. £100,000 proved to be totally inadequate; the first estimate of the provisional committee's secretary was that at least £170,000 would be needed. More seriously, many supporters were failing to produce the monies they had promised. These were anti-Catholics, who had seen the College as designed to defend the Church of England against papism. They had already been dismayed by a decision not to question students about their religious beliefs, and were infuriated the following year when the Duke of Wellington and Peel, for political reasons, gave their support to the Catholic Emancipation Bill.

On 14 March 1829 the most prominent of them, the Earl of Winchilsea, published a letter which accused the Duke of supporting the College 'as a blind' so that he might more effectively 'carry on his insidious design … for the introduction of popery into every department of state'. When Winchilsea refused to apologise the Duke challenged him to a duel, and at 8 a.m. on 21 March 1829 they met in Battersea Fields. 'Damn it! Don't stick him up so near the ditch,' the Duke told his second. 'If I hit him he will tumble in.' But he missed, at which Winchilsea fired in the air. Winchilsea then did apologise, but neither he nor many of his supporters renewed their financial promises, with the result that the College from the start was seriously short of funds.

Money apart, the provisional committee's most urgent problem was to find premises for the College, and it considered over 20 proposals, one of them the purchase of Buckingham Palace, another to build on the part of Regent's Park at that time occupied by the Royal Botanical Gardens. Eventually the Government offered two acres of derelict land between the Strand and the Thames, immediately to the east of Somerset House.

The disadvantages of this site were clear from the start. A letter to the *Mechanics' Magazine* in November 1829 described it as 'probably the very worst that could have been selected in the whole metropolis or its vicinity'. It was 'within about five minutes' walk' of 'five theatres' and of all the 'other sinks of iniquity which derive their support from these celebrated schools of morality'. Wych Street, which opened immediately opposite the site's Strand entrance, was a notorious haunt of prostitutes. And in this short stretch of the Strand between the Law Courts and Waterloo Bridge there were 29 public houses, the Somerset Arms actually forming part of the site's Strand frontage.

One incident gives the flavour of the area in which the School was set. A month after it opened two men arrived with a body which they offered to sell to the assistant of the College's Professor of Anatomy for dissection. The assistant became suspicious and sent for the police. Subsequently the men confessed that they had murdered the corpse, an Italian street-singer aged 14 (well known to the boys because he often performed at the College gates), by lowering him head down into a well, and admitted to selling almost a thousand other bodies, but claimed that this was the only one they had killed. A crowd of 30,000 watched their hanging.

Furthermore this narrow strip of land reaching from the Strand to the river was far too small. The playground eventually provided for the boys of the School, soon to number over 500, measured a mere 20 by 6 yards. The College would also be required to create a Thames frontage in keeping with the frontage which William Chambers had given Somerset House, and to buy and demolish two houses to enlarge the site where it faced east on to Strand Lane and two others to create an entrance from the Strand. All this, together with brickwork to correct the site's slope, was to cost £34,000.

Dr Major in 1834, drawn by a pupil.

Nevertheless the Provisional Committee agreed to the site as the best it could find and, after turning down John Nash as its architect (who offered to work free), chose instead Robert Smirke, designer of the British Museum, no doubt because he was the architect in charge of Somerset House. The building which Smirke erected ran north and south along the whole of Strand Lane, leaving an open space – quadrangle would be too grand a word – between itself and Somerset House. Work began on 10 September 1829 and was sufficiently finished for the College and School to open just over two years later. The part of the building allotted to the School was the basement.

Meanwhile under the Royal Charter of August 1829 the Provisional Committee had handed over its responsibilities to a Council of 22, among whom D'Oyly was again prominent. It was the Council which, in April the following year (1830), advertised for a headmaster for the School. The only known applicant was the Revd John Richardson Major, 31-year-old Headmaster of the Foundation School, Wisbech, Cambridgeshire. At first he did not satisfy the Council and only after it had re-advertised and found no one better did it offer him the position.

Major instantly wrote to the Council asking a dozen questions. Astonishingly, he did not yet know when he was to start work, whether he would be given a house, how many classes he would personally have to teach, how many assistant masters he would be given, what holidays the school would have or the age limits of its pupils. He had apparently not even been told where the School would be sited or whether it would take boarders for he added that a boarding school needed extensive premises for its pupils' exercise and how could these be provided in central London. All this on 27 November when the building of the College with its basement for the day boys of the School had been going forward for two and a half months.

The front of King's College London, 1833. The School occupied the basement. Architect Robert Smirke.

More significantly, he asked whether 'the general system of tuition and discipline' would be left to the discretion of the Headmaster. Though the Council seems to have accepted that these were his responsibilities, it maintained a detailed control over the School. Major had to obtain its approval for every textbook he used and even its permission to start a library. In one sense he was to be the School's great nineteenth-century Head Master, holding the position for 35 years, but he never achieved the freedom to manage his own school which other great headmasters began to achieve from the 1850s.

The Council fixed Major's salary at five guineas a year for every pupil up to 100, four guineas for each additional pupil, and 100 guineas for any that he boarded at his own house, sums which seemed generous even with numbers of 150 (the Bishop of London's lowest estimate), but which were to prove much more so. At one time he was receiving about £1,600 a year, twice the salary of the Principal of the College.

A year later, on Saturday, 8 October 1831, the College and its School were ceremonially opened, the Bishop of London preaching 'a very impressive sermon' (*The Times*) in the College chapel which was the central feature of its first floor

12

and seated 800. The event was somewhat overshadowed by the House of Lords' rejection the previous day of the Second Reform Bill, an event which made the country's bishops (who had voted against it) less than popular, and was further dampened by rain. Nevertheless the following Monday the School's first 85 pupils duly arrived.

The great majority were the sons of professional fathers (one of the first head boys was Thomas Hatchard, son of the founder of the Piccadilly bookshop) and the rapid rise in the School's numbers (to 350 by November 1834) shows how badly people of this class had been wanting such a school. During the 15 years which followed the Napoleonic Wars many of the schools they might have used had decayed. In and around London, Highgate School had only 19 boys in 1838, Westminster only 67 in 1841, and in 1824 St Paul's was below its statutory number of 153. These numbers reflected the low esteem in which such schools were now held. Outside London there were, of course, the seven 'great' or public schools, but they were essentially for boarders, inconvenient before the railway boom of the late 1830s and expensive. They were also beginning to be seen as uncivilised places, a reputation which Dr. Arnold was attempting at exactly this time (1828–41) to correct at Rugby.

Most of the parents of these original 85 boys lived within walking distance of the school, often in the City above their places of business. Those of Henry Crisp (1831–2) lived next door in Somerset House, where his father worked in the Navy Pay Office. Only 12 had homes so far away that they boarded, either with Major who at first lived at Clapham, or with the Second Master, the Revd Joseph Edwards.

The gin shop next to the entrance to KCS. One of a series of pictures drawn by boys and inserted in the Autograph Books of 1834 and 1835, which were signed by every boy attending the school.

Above: *The entrance of the college in 1831* (The Mirror, *15 October 1831*). *A picture of the entrance taken in the 1930s* (right) *shows surprisingly little change over the years.*

Frederick Manning (1831–6) remembered the excitement on that first Monday morning.

> As soon as the portal was opened, there was a rush. Happening to be young and small, I think I got under the legs of some tall fellows, and if I was not the first to enter, I was certainly one of the first three or four. I was a little disconcerted to find that our School was to be downstairs on the basement storey, in the kitchen as some said, or, according to others, in the cellar.

The principal feature of this basement was a corridor 10 ft wide running the whole of the College's 300 ft length. It was permanently dark, requiring gas lamps in autumn and winter, lamps which would turn blue or fail during London fogs so that candles, one for every pair of boys, had to be issued. Several of the classrooms which opened off the corridor were floored with flags, making the atmosphere permanently dank. Down this gloomy tunnel the larger boys presently learned to charge with linked arms, scattering or overrunning the smaller.

14

Things were not improved by the smell of drains (the Thames was still a sewer for a million Londoners) and by the stench from the nearby dissecting room of the College's medical department which sometimes forced the Lower Sixth to abandon its classroom. As for the view, the Revd Sabine Baring-Gould, later to be the author of 159 books and to write 'Onward Christian Soldiers', remembered that what windows there were looked into 'the hard paved playground, surrounded by high stone walls, in which not a blade of grass showed, and not a leaf quivered in the air … the boys in the playground appeared destitute of buoyancy of life, crushed by the subterranean nature of the school and the appalling ugliness of the buildings'. He might have added that one of the houses across Strand Lane looking down on the playground was a brothel, at the windows of which its prostitutes would display themselves for the entertainment of the boys.

The school day for these early boys was condensed. Between 9 a.m. when they arrived until 1 p.m. there was only a ten-minute break at 11 o'clock. The school then offered lunch, at first organised by two masters, then by a succession of caterers, but the food was often disgusting and so inefficiently distributed that by the time some boys were served they would have only five minutes left in which to eat their meal. As a result only a small number took school lunches (29 in 1837, out of nearly 400) the rest dining at local taverns or waiting until 4 o'clock (3 o'clock in winter) when school ended and they could eat at home.

The disadvantage of such a timetable was that it left little opportunity for games or for school societies. On the other hand it also left no time for one common feature of boarding schools. At King's there was little secret homosexuality. What there was developed because boys were divided not by age but by merit, the young but clever put into classes with the much older. Frederic Harrison (1843–8 to become a well-known lawyer, journalist and historian) went into the Lower Sixth at the age of $11\frac{1}{2}$. There he

> struggled desperately for a time against the girl's name which was imposed on me; but … I had to submit, and for some two or three years I never heard myself spoken of in school … except as 'Fan' … I was habitually treated as a girl. A boy who struck me in earnest would have been pounded by a dozen fists … If I called for help, half a dozen fellows would come to orders, and in a half-joking way do what they were told.

He added that he took no harm from the experience, perhaps because 'the universal acceptance of my position … took away from its dangers'.

At first the boys were divided into two classes, one taught by Major, one by Edwards. Large classes were typical of the period – Major subsequently claimed that he used to teach 60 or 70 without difficulty. But the growth of the School soon made more classes and masters essential. William Ince (1834–41, later Professor of Divinity at Oxford) remembered that there were six, the top class divided into the Upper and Lower Sixth. By then 'All the boys were taught Latin and Greek and elementary mathematics, and French also I believe. German was optional, and taught at somewhat inconvenient hours in the afternoon.'

The School's curriculum had been ahead of its time from the start. Besides religious instruction and the classics, the Royal Charter had prescribed that

The gate at the end of the long corridor which ran the full length of the subterranean School, drawn by a boy and entitled 'abandon hope all ye who enter here'.

The French master, Brasseur, 1830s, here described as 'A haberdasher from Rouens' (Autograph Book, 1833).

"300 lines of Virgil,... Sirrah!"

"I'll make you hate yourself Sir!"

Revd John Fearnley (Autograph Book, 1834).

The Greenwich railroad as envisaged by a KCS boy in 1836. William Treloar (1854–8), future Lord Mayor of London, travelled to the school on this railway.

mathematics, arithmetic, English literature, and English composition should be taught, as well as 'some modern languages when desired'. The School's first prospectus had been even more ambitious and added writing, ancient and modern history and geography, and elocution. It continued, 'The German, Spanish and Italian Languages, the Principles and Practice of Commerce, Natural Philosophy, drawing, and the other branches of knowledge and science, will be taught out of course, to those who are desirous of instruction.' At Rugby in these years Arnold was adding nothing except a little history to the Latin and Greek taught there – as at all other grammar and public schools. At first King's boys paid four guineas extra a year for 'out-of-course' subjects (the basic fee was 18 guineas, reduced to 15 for the nominees of shareholders or of donors of £50 or more), but during the School's third year the Council made German and drawing free.

Major himself was a committed classicist – he had published a Greek dictionary which was widely used until eclipsed in 1843 by Liddell and Scott's. According to James Heath (1845–52) 'Dr Major … held with supreme conviction the view that the one thing worth doing in life was to study the Greek and Latin Classics.' But he was no great teacher. Harrison remembered that 'we did what we liked, read novels and poetry during lessons … I worked well, and with great enjoyment, but much in my own way.' Even at the classics Harrison thought him 'a very moderate scholar of the old school'. On the other hand he was generally much liked. He was a short man with a big head, known to the boys as Gog, perhaps derived from his own name via Magog. 'It was only on entering his class,' Martin Irving (1842–9) remembered, 'that we boys began to understand and appreciate Dr Major. He was not indeed one of those teachers who inspire enthusiasm, he was not even brilliant. But what we could not help admiring was the conscientious, infinite laboriousness of the man, his unwearied diligence.'

Though Edwards was, according to Ince, 'a man of fine scholarship', he was not much of an improvement as a teacher, but 'far too indolent in his proper work. Much of his school time was occupied in preparing small schoolbooks adapted from the German, and I am afraid that his class spent many idle hours under his too easy superintendence.' Other things distracted him; he was 'most ingenious in technical appliances and manufactures', and obtained patents for some of his inventions. Manning remembered him as 'much given to the violin, the pleasant sounds whereof not infrequently stole from his private room'. It is not surprising that Edwards was demoted in 1851, when a Vice-Master was made his superior.

This future Vice-Master, the Revd John Fearnley, arrived as Third Master in 1832. Known to the boys as Infernal Jack, he was remembered by Sydney Thelwall (1848) as 'a burly Yorkshireman – supposed to be the strictest master in the school, but just withal, and capable'. According to Ince, 'His massive frame, his strong hand in giving boys occasionally a box on the ear or dragging them on to a sort of stool of penance, and sundry mysterious stories about incidents in his life, all tended to inspire terror.' William Treloar (1854–8, future Lord Mayor of London), who would travel to school in an open truck of the London–Greenwich railway, remembered that once while reading to Fearnley he met the word 'abdomen', and had to admit that he didn't know its meaning. 'Fearnley then struck me with his big Yorkshire fist in the stomach and said, "That is your abdomen, and don't forget it."'

In 1831 the only other regular master was Frederick Ribbans, teacher of drawing, writing, and arithmetic. He was remembered by Ince as 'a universal favourite'. He was also an inspiring teacher; in the early 1830s the boys presented him with several volumes of sketches, poems, and jokes, one described on its title page by its five authors as 'A Small Tribute of Their Respect and Esteem'. The sketches show much talent as well as giving a vivid picture of the London in which the School was set.

Gift book to Ribbans, the drawing master, 1834.

In 1837, however, Ribbans was accused of selling school stationery, and despite a petition from Major, Edwards and two other masters, was dismissed by the Council. This was typical. It not only underpaid its masters but regularly failed to support them when in trouble. In 1835 another early master, George Blake, was imprisoned for debt and dismissed. The following year the same happened to his successor, Abraham Newland. Debt was, of course, criminal at the time and the Council was defending the School's reputation, but it was just as stern with Edwards, dismissing him in 1853 for leaving his class unattended during certain Tuesday and Friday periods in order to act as chaplain to the Fishmongers' Company.

The Council nevertheless often received as many as 40 applications when it advertised teaching positions, and was able to choose well-qualified staff. One, Thomas Cockayne, a Cambridge Wrangler, became the leading philologist of his time. Lessons in fencing were given by Signor Angelo, Fencing Master to His Majesty's Forces. Italian was taught by Gabriele Rossetti, father of Dante Gabriel, and William Michael, both of whom came to the School in 1837. And to take over the teaching of drawing from Ribbans the Council recruited the best known of all the School's early masters, the water-colourist John Sell Cotman.

Revd G. Blake, Fourth Master, who was later incarcerated in Fleet Prison for debt and eventually drowned himself (Autograph Book, 1835).

Cotman was given a modest basic salary of £100, with the addition of £1 for every pupil over 100 who attended his classes. At once he attracted 250, the following year 284, and for the first time in his life was free from financial worry. Neither William Rossetti nor the future well-known painter Stephen Pearce (1834–6), thought him a good teacher and he had so much trouble with the Fifth Form that Edwards had to attend its drawing classes to help him keep order, but in 1838 he told the College Secretary that he loved his boys and believed he received nothing but respect from them. Of those he taught nine became practising artists, ten architects.

REV — G — BLAKE, MA.

If Fearnley occasionally boxed a boy's ears, this was an exception to another remarkable early feature of King's. From the start and throughout Major's regime corporal punishment was forbidden. To compare this with a single example from elsewhere, in the late 1840s a boy at Marlborough, caned by a master, had to be taken to the school doctor to have pieces of his shirt picked out of his back. In 1833 Major replied to a letter in the *Weekly Dispatch*, 'I have in no instance inflicted corporal punishment on a Pupil … the Under-Masters in this Department are not allowed a cane or any other instrument of punishment in their rooms.' Without canes or the threat of flogging by the Head Master the

Fighting involving boys and a master, picture by Dante Gabriel Rossetti, 1830s.

'A cherub in purgatory', typical of the punning pictures of the time (Autograph Book, 1834).

assistant masters were forced to resort to enormous impositions. In 1840 Butcher of the Upper First was ordered to learn Pope's Messiah by heart for ill-treating Robson of the Lower First; and Fly Smith to learn six pages of Chronicles by heart for falsehood, stealing a pencil, and cutting a boy's cap.

The playground in particular gave opportunities for misbehaviour. Major and his ten assistant masters sent the Council a round robin in 1839, explaining that it was surfaced with 'loose stones, and so presents a continual temptation to the pupils to indulge in the dangerous practice of throwing stones at each other'. He eventually persuaded the Council to reduce and stagger the lunch break (which he described as 'an uproar the most deafening and disturbing') and to instruct the school porter to clean and water the playground once a week.

It was in the playground that the famous riot of 1848 began. Though the Chartist riot had occurred three and a half months earlier (April 1848) there is no reason for thinking that the event at King's was political, nor for comparing it with such late school riots as those at Marlborough in 1851 or at King's School, Canterbury, in 1859. These were revolts against the school and its masters, that at King's College School a mass battle between two groups of boys.

It had become the habit of the Upper Sixth (numbering 24) to commandeer the playground for a form of rackets, and this had produced growing resentment among the boys of the Middle and Lower Sixth. At one o'clock on 21 July, when the masters in charge had left the School for lunch, the boys of these much larger forms attacked the rackets players.

There followed a violent battle in which rackets were used. Booth, the porter, a stout, one-armed, retired soldier, shut himself in his office and Major remained in his classroom. Sydney Thelwall (1848), who watched as a young boy, remembered that even Fearnley, who arrived in cap and gown, retreated

as he seemed to feel that he was helpless … So the fight raged. And how it would have ended I cannot tell but for the arrival of half-past one. So those young masters who had gone out would come in. Among these were 'Tommy' [Markby] and the Head Master's son, young Major; the former not long come … from Cambridge, the latter from Oxford. And now was shown what two young men neither of them much above middle height, but both strongly built, well-knit men, can do when their minds are made up, and they have right on their side … these two dons plunged straight into the heart of the conflict, and began pinioning this hero and that without regard to standing. 'Your name and class, Sir,' was the unwelcome greeting with which one of the strongest and fiercest of the warriors found himself met – I had the tale from his own lips – as, finding his vigorous elbows suddenly held in a vice by a still more masterful grip, he faced round … and encountered the keen grey eyes of 'Tommy'.

Major's 35 years fall naturally into two parts. During his first 18 years the School thrived to an extent that neither he nor the Council can have hoped. In February 1834 the Council ordered a limit of 400 boys, but six years later, during which time the College had come to rely on the School for revenue, it removed this limit. In 1843 numbers peaked at 519; in 1846 and 1847 they were still above 500.

One result was that the School required more classrooms; in January 1832 it took over a classroom on the first floor from the College, in November an additional classroom in the basement, and at the same time a large basement hall as a recreation room for use in wet weather. Four years later it acquired the College's dining-room and medical room for further classrooms.

The success of the College as a whole was recognised on 22 June 1843 when it was visited by Prince Albert. After the boys had been drilled by Fearnley they were

'Three miles from KCS' (Autograph Book, 1834).

> posted on the staircase to the left on entering from the street. The professors afterwards came, and last Prince Albert. The Royal Standard was hoisted outside the building. A Latin oration was given, after which the Prince, accompanied by Mr Lonsdale [Principal of the College] walked up the staircase … to the museum. He was cheered the whole way. After the oration, those who had learnt to sing, sang 'God Save the Queen, God save the Prince'.

By 1850, however, numbers at the School had shrunk to 423, as a result, Major claimed, of the 'large number of good schools that have sprung up in the vicinity of London'. It was then that the Council decided on a radical modernisation of the School's already relatively modern curriculum. It would now be divided into two separate sides, one classical, the other 'practical', or as it was soon named, the 'Division of Modern Instruction'. Again King's was ahead. The next earliest public schools to start modern sides were Marlborough and Rossall in 1854 and the majority did not follow until many years later.

The Division of Modern Instruction would, in the Council's words, 'afford more suitable education to a large class of boys likely in after life to be engaged in other than classical studies'. The boys saw the subdivision somewhat differently. Henry Salter (1856–8), afterwards a successful doctor, marksman, and dog-breeder, remembered that

A school certificate from 1832.

> In the school there was an A department, for boys going into the professions, and a B department for those intended for trade. The two were always at loggerheads, the As looking down on the Bs, and there was a good deal of antagonism, with fighting every day. Among the most redoubtable warriors, who fought almost as a band of brothers, were those known as the Hoi Sloiteroi – Ted Pollock, Jim Connor, and my humble self.

A scene near KCS drawn by E. H. Corbould, subsequently instructor in painting to the Royal Family (Autograph Book, 1835).

Trap-ball (Autograph Book, 1834).

Salter's addiction to fighting continued and in 1861 he lost an eye at Epsom races in a quarrel with the English heavyweight boxing champion.

In 1855 the School appointed its first science master, Charles Tomlinson FRS, FCS, ahead of all other public schools except the City of London School. Major apparently approved.

> Once a week [a boy remembered] we were summoned for one hour to a lecture upstairs in the College proper … Dr Major … sat in front, in the post of danger when explosive experiments … were being performed. We used to watch his anxious face whenever Mr Tomlinson, filling jars and bottles with unseen gases, announced that a violent explosion would immediately be produced. If the explosion came off, well and good; if not, the disappointing result was greeted with ironic cheers, which the doctor, grateful perhaps for his own escape, did not suppress.

Major's wide interests are confirmed by his early enthusiasm for photography. In 1856 he became founder secretary of the London Photographic Society. The College was the first of any college or school in the country to teach photography, and the same year held an exhibition of photographs in its Great Hall which was 'thronged by all the notables of literature and science in the metropolis' (*Notes and Queries*).

From the School's opening Major had also encouraged the writing of English verse, keeping a book in which the best poems of the year were entered; and as early as 1833 the boys produced a magazine, entitled *Juvenilia*, its contents more earnest and learned than the official magazine first published in the 1870s. In 1850 the Literary Union was formed, to become in practice a debating society. During Major's time prizes were awarded for such natural history exhibits as 'Best Herbarium'; both the future director of Kew Gardens, William Thiselton-Dyer (1858–61) and the future director of the Botanical Gardens, Ceylon, Henry Trimen (1855–9), started their careers with botanical rambles from the school.

Not surprisingly, King's, without playing fields and with only short breaks in its day, was less advanced at games. James Heath (1845–52) remembered that boys 'played no games … each one lived at home in his father's house; and our only opportunity of measuring ourselves with our fellow creatures was in the classroom during school hours'.

This was not entirely accurate; Ince remembered that even in the 1830s the boys of Major's and Fearnley's houses formed cricket clubs which would play at St John's Wood or Kennington Oval; in the 1840s Frederic Harrison remembered playing at Lord's, and Henry Preece (1845–8) claimed to have been the School's cricket captain. In 1841 the Council paid for 'a Fives Bench and a Tennis Bench' in the playground. And as early as 1839 and 1840 Old Boys earned Oxford blues. The majority of boys, however, played no organised games, even if they 'had a great recourse in continual fights, and out of these they got almost as much exercise and enjoyment' (Treloar).

Eventually in 1860 there arrived at the School the sort of athletic cleric who was a common feature of schools of the time. The Revd James Kingdon persuaded the Council to contribute £10 towards a cricket club, which played at the Eton and Middlesex ground near Primrose Hill, against schools like Merchant Taylors' and St Paul's. He also encouraged rowing on the Thames, helping boys to buy 'an old Westminster "eight"'. 'This we used to launch at the Feather, Wandsworth, rowing leisurely up river until we had enough, and then went home for our quarter, where we arrived, much to the astonishment of four boatmen, who, having watched our performance in getting under weigh, naturally never expected to see us again.' But by 1866 Kingdon was gone and Major told the Council, 'since Mr Kingdon left us, we have not had a muscular Master to take part or interest in Cricket Matches'.

The part that work rather than games played at the School may explain the remarkable number of distinguished Old Boys it produced in Major's time. No fewer than 99 appear in the *Dictionary of National Biography*. If Dante Gabriel Rossetti is the only one to remain a household name, many others are still known to those in their fields, for example Edward Barry (1845–8), assistant to his father, Charles, who rebuilt the House of Commons (when it burned down in 1834 the boys were given the day off to watch); George Saintsbury (1858–63), distinguished Edinburgh Professor of English, better remembered today for his *Notes on a Cellar-Book* (he would claim that when offered a glass of sherry before supper he could tell whether the bottle had just been opened or opened at lunchtime); Henry Fawcett, FRS (1849–51), blinded in a shooting accident at 25, Gladstone's Postmaster-General and the introducer of the parcels post; and Treloar, founder of Lord Mayor Treloar's Cripples' Hospital and College, which still flourishes.

Robert Pritchett (1843–5) was a stranger philanthropist. First, an inventor (a bullet he devised earned him a £1,000 government reward), then a painter and illustrator who contributed to *Punch*, also a well-known yachtsman and an authority on ancient armour, he is remembered today as one of the founders of the Working Men's College. A more significant technologist was William Preece (1845–8), Engineer-in-Chief to the Post Office, who in 1876 first brought Bell telephone receivers into the country.

Pen and ink sketch by an anonymous pupil of Cotman, 1834, based on the title of a well-known eighteenth century poem.

Burning down of the Houses of Parliament in 1834. The whole school went to watch (sketch by S. Pearce, a pupil, subsequently a sporting and group artist).

21

Ten boys became bishops or archbishops, while in total 362 took holy orders, an interesting contrast with the fewer than 20 who became Members of Parliament.

Though the fathers of the boys were predominantly middle-class professionals, 62 Old Boys later won titles and ten holders of hereditary titles sent their sons. Others found the School a convenient place to cater for their mistakes. Baron Lytton (the novelist Edward Bulwer-Lytton) sent his illegitimate son. So did the 12th Duke of Gordon, inventing for him a non-existent title: Lord Huntley.

Despite its modern side the School's decline continued; under Major it never again had 500 boys, and by 1865 had only 367. One year, as an economy, the Council imposed a $2\frac{1}{2}$ per cent cut in masters' salaries. Eight years later the cut was increased to 3 per cent. From 1850 it became increasingly dissatisfied with the School's teaching and discipline, and finally in February 1866 it set up a committee to investigate both the College and the School.

About the School the Committee reported that the masters

> all say that they are generally able to maintain the discipline in their own classes, but that the general discipline is very defective; that exeats are granted by the Head Master on the mere application of the boys, without any reference to the Masters, and in many cases where they certainly would not grant them; and they evidently feel that they are not supported in matters of discipline by the Head Master.

Several masters acknowledged the help Fearnley had given them in maintaining discipline, 'sometimes by judicious interference in matters more strictly within the province of the Head Master'.

About Major the report concluded, 'as at every school, the time must come when the most able scholar becomes too old to retain the management and teaching of boys'. For a long time Major had been an able master of a school which retained a high reputation and had sent many excellent scholars to the universities, but 'the time has come when a gentleman who took his degree forty-seven years ago ought to be relieved from the duties of teaching'.

Major seems to have had no idea that he would be asked to resign. 'The very brief notice which the Committee of KC condescended to give me,' he began his reply. Not surprisingly, when it asked him to stay one more term he refused. In 1866 its verdict on Major may have been fair, but it was typical of the lack of consideration with which it had treated him for the previous 35 years.

It granted him an annual pension of £300, but during the following years he frequently had to write to ask for this to be promptly paid. The private school he started at Ramsgate failed, and for a time he held an ill-paid curacy in Cambridgeshire. His son and son-in-law both died before him and when he too died, ten years after being dismissed from King's, he left not a penny.

Dr Major in 1860.

22

CHAPTER TWO

Maclear - Discipline and Success
1866–1880

In 1860 a 27-year-old Cambridge graduate, the Revd George Frederick Maclear, had come to King's as master of the Lower Fifth on the classics side. Six years later, on 29 May 1866, shortly after Major had been forced to resign, Maclear also resigned, giving ill-health and pressure of other duties as his reasons. That autumn, when Major had refused to stay an extra term, the Council appointed Maclear, now apparently recovered, as temporary head, and soon afterwards chose him from 12 well-qualified applicants to be permanent Head Master.

Underlying and perhaps explaining these somewhat odd events was a close friendship between Maclear and the Council's Secretary, J. W. Cunningham; possibly Maclear's resignation was part of their plan to put him in a better position to apply for the headship. Certainly soon after he had been interviewed by the Council for the permanent post he wrote to Cunningham, 'Allow me to take this opportunity of thanking you for your kindness during the affair.'

Maclear was not only a man of energy and firm opinions, but of experience, having acted as external examiner at various other schools. He had also written classical and religious textbooks (theology had been his subject at Cambridge). From the start he behaved as if he meant to stay, making changes which his six years at the school had shown him to be needed. He agreed with the Council's committee that discipline was bad, in particular that boys were leaving school premises illegally during the day. He had locks for which boys had obtained keys changed, and told the school porter to be more diligent. After two years he introduced corporal punishment, first for junior boys then for all.

He also made a fundamental change to the School by adding a Lower Division. It had been clear for a long time that there were too few young boys. Most arrived from some previous school and though some stayed until they went

George Frederick Maclear,
Head Master 1866–80.

to Oxford or Cambridge, a large number left at 16 to go into commerce or the professions. As a result the School was middle heavy, and at the same time lacked a reliable source of new pupils. As long ago as 1834 one master had suggested that it should found its own preparatory school; Maclear's new Lower Division was a substitute.

There was no immediate improvement in numbers which continued to fall, reaching 357 in 1869. Even in 1872 when they had risen to 519 there were only 36 boys aged 12 or less. By the end of Maclear's time, however, the boys of the Lower Division were almost a third of the total.

To take charge of the Lower Division Maclear appointed a popular housemaster, the Revd George Rust. His name, one Old Boy wrote, 'should ever command respect at King's'. Rust tried to remedy the School's lack of playing fields by gathering his junior boys in their spare time to 'practise the noble game' (cricket), but the scheme collapsed when he died suddenly in 1874.

Most significant of Maclear's other changes was his revitalisation of the School's Division of Modern Instruction. This had in practice become a dumping ground for boys not intelligent enough to progress up the classics side. On the one hand he insisted that all boys on the modern side do some Latin and English, on the other he grouped them according to their particular abilities – in mathematics or English for example. To take charge of the modern side he appointed the Revd John Twentyman (Vice-Master since Fearnley's resignation in 1866). As one assistant he gave him C. H. Cunningham, son of the Council's Secretary, doubtless a reward for the father's help.

Cunningham, the father, probably continued to help Maclear to get his way with the Council, but Maclear also helped himself: he was one of the earliest Head Masters partially to free himself from being automatically the full-time teacher of the classics Sixth Form, reserving three mornings a week on which to 'deal with the general direction and supervision of the School'. He had power, too, since the College was still in financial difficulties (on average during the 1870s it received £5,000 a year from the School), power which increased as numbers rose, eventually reaching 635 in the summer of 1880 when he resigned.

Again the School needed more space, something Maclear argued strongly for in a pamphlet which the Council printed in 1873. Some was provided by creating two new classrooms out of one end of the gymnasium, but the Council, with debts of £30,000, had no money for building, even if it could have found space. Its problems had been compounded by the sudden collapse in 1869 of the entire roof of the dining hall, carrying its floor into the kitchen below. The disaster happened at 8.15 a.m. and no one was hurt. Excavations for the construction of the Victoria Embankment were blamed.

In his pamphlet Maclear also argued against insistence on the transfer of boys at 16 from the School to the College, still in theory compulsory. He had found that the boys who wanted to transfer were scientists or prospective doctors. Parents of boys going to Oxford or Cambridge preferred them to stay with teachers they knew, under the School's discipline, and so did their teachers who would, he believed, be seriously discouraged since they were 'naturally interested in the progress and success of their boys'.

Opposite page: KCS pupils in the College workshop, 1872.

In Maclear's time games continued to be restricted by the school's lack of playing fields. It did its best, however, to match the athleticism which was beginning to dominate the country's public schools, establishing a Rugby Football Club (with Maclear as president) which was soon playing matches against Dulwich, St Paul's, University College School, and King's College itself. On 1 February 1873 'The College as usual turned up short of men.' The same year the Boat Club was refounded (Maclear as president). Rule 10 read, 'That a fine not exceeding 2*s. 6d.* be inflicted on any member for gross misconduct or language, and that this fine be fixed at the discretion of the captain of the boat.'

More of a general School occasion was the annual meeting of the Athletics Club (Maclear president), held on the site of the future Chelsea football ground in West Brompton. On 7 June 1873 between four and five thousand spectators attended. On 14 July 1879 there were 30 events, starting with drop-kicking and place-kicking, ending with a quarter mile servants' race and consolation race.

In the same years other extra-curricular activities began to match those of the country's boarding public schools. There was now a King's College Junior Choral Society (patron Maclear), meeting twice a week and giving occasional concerts of glees and choruses. The School chaplain, the Revd Henry Belcher (1871–86), remembered how the Head Master would attend the rehearsals of the English play.

> Of one scene in particular he was never weary. It was the famous scene in *The Critic* where the two nieces are about to slay, or be slain, and Don Whiskerandos is at deadlocks ... Now, the boys ... might as well have been marionettes, so far as acting goes ... while the nieces had voices like a penny whistle. Never was there worse acting on the British stage, as acting! But we agreed that for farce the unconscious comedy of the performers was unsurpassable. Maclear ... would ask for them to do the scene over and over again: and laugh! He laughed till the tears rolled down his face.

Strangely, the boy of the time who was to become best known, the painter Walter Sickert (1875–8), founder of the Camden Group, left King's intending to

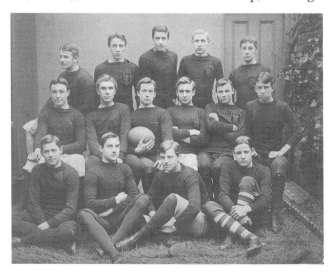

The Rugby team of 1880–81. Reginald McKenna, later Chancellor of the Exchequer, is second from the left in the back row. KCS was one of the first schools to feature Rugby, which started there in 1863.

become an actor. At the School he played leading parts in scenes from various Shakespeare plays, and in 1880, during the three years he spent on the stage, he returned to give a performance of Clarence's dream from *Richard III*.

'This recitation was one of the features of the day; in it Sickert surpassed himself, and evoked the greatest burst of applause heard during the evening ... We hope he may meet with similar success in his professional career.'

Sickert's contemporary, Joseph Crawhall (1877–8), though expelled from King's for indecency, was also to become a well-known painter, founder member of the Glasgow School, suggesting that art was well taught in Maclear's time. And the School's best known writer of the period, Thomas Guthrie (1872–5, pen name F. Anstey) had a precocious talent for drawing. When he performed in Aristophanes' *The Frogs*, he illustrated his text with remarkable groups of frogs dancing on their hind legs. About his performance Anstey wrote that after his first 15 lines he forgot his part and was forced to repeat them with different intonations.

Anstey's novel, *Vice Versa*, in which a father is transformed into a schoolboy to re-experience 'the best days of his life', was based on a preparatory school which he had attended before King's, but one character was easily recognised as the King's German master, Gustav Reinicke. In another novel, *The Giant's Robe*, he described King's at the moment its school day ended:

> Even if you went down the broad stairs to the school entrance and along the basement, where the bulk of the classrooms was situated, there was only a faint hum to be heard behind the numerous doors - until the red-waistcoated porter came out of his lodge and rang the big bell which told that the day's work was over.

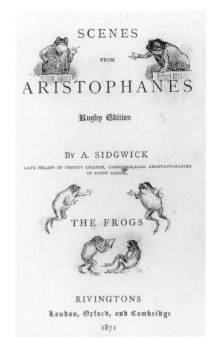

Above and below left: *Pictures by Thomas Anstey Guthrie illustrating Aristophanes'* The Frogs. *Guthrie subsequently became a comic author under the name F. Anstey.*

Then nervous people who found themselves by any chance in the long dark corridors experienced an unpleasant sensation, as of a demon host in high spirits being suddenly let loose to do their will ... then door after door opened and hordes of boys plunged out with wild shrieks of liberty, to scamper madly down the echoing flagstones.

For half an hour after that the place was a Babel of unearthly yells, whistles, and scraps of popular songs, with occasional charges and scuffles and a constant tramp of feet.

In his autobiography Anstey described the Fourth Form master, the Revd William Hayes, known to the boys as Lobster or alternatively Billy.

His face distinctly suggested one of the grotesque figures that used to be constructed out of lobster claws and embellished by a fringe of white hair and a black velvet toque. His eyes were grey and quick, like a parrot's, his nose prominent, his mouth thin-lipped, and his complexion a clear healthy brick-red ...

As a rule I escaped serious trouble in Billy's form, but there was one day of disaster. He caught me prompting a neighbour in distress, gave me a hundred lines, and sent me to the Detention Room, with the words 'For prompting' written large at the top of my imposition sheet.

I had not been writing long when Dr Maclear, the Head Master, entered majestically, and I gave myself up for lost, knowing well that prompting was a swishable offence.

He came up to my seat – which I should have liked to crawl under – looked over my shoulder, and read the fatal words.

And then, just when I was expecting an invitation to his private room, he passed me in silence.

Other extra-curricular activities still included those of the School's Literary Union, founded 20 years earlier, partly at the instigation of John Worgan Festing (1852–6, future Bishop of St Albans). In November 1853 Festing had read a paper to the Union entitled, 'The Effect of Religion and Politics on the Hair and Beard'. At first its meetings usually took the form of a mock court, with judge, jury, plaintiff and defendant, but soon became conventional debates. In November 1872 it voted 13 to 6 that public education was preferable to private. Later the same month it voted 15 to 3 against the building of a tunnel under the English Channel – a result perhaps influenced by the recent defeat of France in the Franco-Prussian War. (Between 1870 and 1872 this defeat brought King's no fewer than 50 boys from the Continent.)

There was also now a Reading Club where 'on any day between one o'clock and half-past and again between three and four ... scores of boys' could be found 'devouring *The Times*, *Daily News*, and *Standard*, admiring our victories in the football columns of the *Field* and *Sportsman* delighting the eyes with the *Graphic*, *Saturday Review*, *Nature*, *Athenaeum*, *Academy*, etc.'.

And by 1873 there was an annual Old Boys' dinner, attended that year by 60 to 70, a number of whom determined 'to have a meeting at an early date' which would 'transform these periodic events into a proper Old Boys' Club'.

Though the dinners almost certainly continued a club was not formed for another eleven years.

Most important of all for catching the flavour of the School at the time, in 1873 a school magazine was launched. 'Knock away the wedge,' the editor ended his first editorial: 'see: she glides from the stocks: the prow is on the brink: she floats: she is off!'

She was a well-produced affair, with an occasional sepia print of impressive clarity. The first (reproduced from a picture by an Old Boy, Arthur Ackland Hunt – 1851–7) showed boys using a lathe operated by a treadle in the metal workshop. Most surprising feature of early numbers was a serial story, 'Slow and Sure', occupying 30 out of the first 120 pages. The remainder carried reports of School matches and society meetings, lists of prize winners and complete school rolls; also occasional readers' letters.

In the third issue 'One of the Librarians' wrote to ask that the library be given fewer novels, of which it already had enough 'to last for a month's hard reading'. He added, 'We should only be too glad to get *Middlemarch* or *Romola*, or any standard works; but for merely sensational books, we shall feel less obliged.'

The three correspondents to the next issue were complainers, the first two about the School food. There were now three ways for boys to buy lunch: in the School dining hall, at a nearby eating-house, or from a pastry cook named Reynolds who was allowed to set up his counter in 'a room in the passage'.

'The pastry that he sells,' wrote Incontentus, 'is, I think, far from being conducive either to health or a good digestion; and yet for want of anything better the majority of the boys are compelled to buy this stuff.'

Front cover of the fifth issue of school magazine 1873.

This food [wrote Fiat Justitia] consists of biscuits, buns, jam tarts, apple tarts, chocolate creams, and other species of sweets, bread and cheese and ham sandwiches. And now, Sir, with the exception of the last two articles … is this the sort of food off which ravenous boys ought to make a repast, however slight? Secondly, if so why should we be made to pay outrageously exorbitant prices… . Now, how can one, situated like your humble servant, do anything else but take and pay? I breakfast before eight o'clock, and do not dine till past 5 p.m., and consequently between my two meals there is an interval of nine hours or more. My case is surely bad enough; but what must those boys undergo who leave home at some time before 7 a.m., and do not get back till 6 p.m.?

On the left-hand side of our handsome entrance [wrote the third correspondent] there stands a mansion build of wood, at a guess I should state its dimensions to be about eleven feet by eight. In this mansion are five basins, to which are attached five taps. At every convenient place there hangs a towel, but since there are only four convenient places there are only four towels. The supply of water is so small that I am not exaggerating in the least when I say it gently trickles out drop by drop. … Such is the accommodation for 530 boys to wash in … it is a worse grievance than the 'food' one gets, because a boy can bring 'sandwiches from home', and so avoid the necessity of poisoning himself on what they call 'eatables'.

The Magazine so hopefully launched in 1873 sank in 1876. The same year one manuscript and one printed issue of *The Clamator* appeared, a slighter affair, but this too failed, perhaps because its principal editor, Arthur Coles (1869–77), was expelled, and it was another four years before a school magazine again began to appear. Four issues of this were published in Maclear's time. Even slimmer and coverless, it described itself as 'conducted' by members of the Literary Union, but included no poems or stories. The second issue admitted that the first had sold disappointingly. 'We have been told', its editorial continued, 'that numbers containing lists of the school are always the most successful', and this is how it filled four of its ten pages. The rest carried accounts of debates, mostly on historical subjects ('Was the execution of Charles I justifiable?') and of football matches.

In his early years Maclear had had to deal with two awkward staff problems. While still temporary Head Master he began to receive complaints from parents about an ancient and indolent housemaster, the Revd Otto Adolphus. He deprived Adolphus of his right to take boarders and instructed him to live nearer the School. Luckily Adolphus was not going to appeal to the Council, Maclear told it, because 'No Head Master can speak with authority to his other Masters if in trifling matters there are to be perpetual appeals.'

If Maclear dealt appropriately with Adolphus, the same cannot be said about the distinguished philologist, Thomas Cockayne, who by 1869 had been a master for 33 years. Cockayne was charged with talking to his class 'unnecessarily of subjects which could only tend to corrupt them'. Defending himself before the Council, he maintained that if he spoke openly about such things it was so that the boys could see clearly the evil effects of vice. When he was dismissed he published a pamphlet, *Mr Cockayne's Narrative*, in which he claimed that Maclear had taken a leading part in the affair. An informer, he wrote, 'had appeared with a misreported conversation of mine; this was afterwards thrown aside, and Mr Maclear, who had leant an ear' to the informer 'was obliged to become prosecutor himself'. Cockayne listed the nine accusations brought against him, one of them that he had explained that the biblical phrase 'Her full time was come' meant nine months. As an appendix he printed eight pages of letters of support from boys and parents, one of whom wrote

Revd Thomas Oswald Cockayne, the leading etymologist of his day, who was dismissed for allegedly using salacious language to his pupils.

> I well remember that you often used to puzzle us boys somewhat by telling us such and such things in history etc., as we ought to have known, but did not; in fact you tried to make us think; and a great deal of good it did some of us. But as touching the matters concerning which the present complaint has been made, I am sure that I never, nor did anyone else in your class while I was there, imbibe from your instruction a single unfit idea.

In 1873, impoverished perhaps by the loss of his teacher's salary, Cockayne shot himself at St Ives, Cornwall.

School life under Maclear was described 40 years later by Harry Preston (1867–71). Some things had changed little since early days. In the playground nothing happened except the 'kicking about indiscriminately a piece of wood'. Though the school day now ended at 3 p.m. to enable boys to go home in good time through the unsavoury nearby streets, not all of them did so. 'Gatti's at the Adelaide Gallery saw many of us afterwards – ice in large glasses – and at Sainsbury's, a chemist close to the school, who sold splendid ice soda drinks from a fountain.'

Preston remembered that half the school had been boarders – an interesting inaccuracy. Boarding was indeed becoming the fashion among the country's middle classes, and this was to prove damaging to King's which had no space for nearby boarding houses, but in fact in 1873 only 75 out of 519 boys lived with various masters.

Sydney Low (1874–5) compared the three most notable teachers of Maclear's time: Maclear himself, Twentyman, and J. W. Hales, one of Maclear's early appointments, later Professor of English Language and Literature at the College.

'For Maclear, a great Head Master, we entertained a deep respect not untinged with fear; he could be rather a formidable personage at times' – a verdict supported by Seymour Chalk (1877–9), who remembered that there was 'a lively dread of Dr Maclear and his hard blue eyes'. John Martin Harvey (1877–9, well-known actor) gives a grim picture of Maclear who birched him 'attended by a smug monitor with a bulbous nose'. Low continued

> But everyone loved 'Tiny' [Twentyman], the most genial, good tempered and urbane of preceptors, with his pleasant manner, his ready smile, his habit of treating us all as if we were much worthier and more capable members of society than we had ever supposed ourselves to be... . He was pretty nearly the best teacher I have ever known. Perhaps not quite the best. I am inclined to assign that place to Professor J. W. Hales ... Hales had a keener and stronger intellect, and his literary knowledge was wider and more critical. But he had also a taste for pungent epigram and did not suffer fools gladly; so that he was not wholly popular.

About Maclear, Hales himself wrote that at first he had been

> much pressed by the severe duties and the heavy responsibilities of his new position. They seemed to him almost overwhelming. Excellent as the record of the School had been, ... some laxities of discipline and arrangement were causing anger. Maclear always in later life referred to that period as one of sore struggle and extreme anxiety. It was, in fact, a critical moment. Was the School to fall or rise? The hour had come to decide this question. Happily, the man, too, had come, and it was Maclear.

Boys of Maclear's time, besides those mentioned, included Reginald McKenna, Cambridge rowing blue, Chancellor of the Exchequer in 1915–16, introducer of National Savings Certificates; and Thomas Lewis, also a Cambridge blue, who in 1877 rowed number two in the only boat race which ended in a draw. As a lawyer Lewis continued to associate with boats, becoming Senior Wreck Commissioner to the Board of Trade.

Maclear did not allow himself to be pushed into impoverished retirement as Major had been. He was still in his late forties when he obtained the position of Warden of St Augustine's, Canterbury, which he held till he died 22 years later.

CHAPTER THREE

Stokoe - Scandal and Hard Times
1880–1889

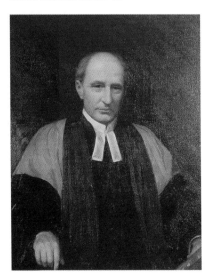

*Revd Thomas Henry Stokoe,
Head Master 1880-9.*

The Revd Thomas Stokoe, Maclear's successor, arrived at King's with excellent qualifications. Aged 46, he had taught at Uppingham under Thring (joint founder of the Headmasters' Conference), then been Second Master at Clifton, virtually establishing the school in the absence of the Headmaster elect. Subsequently, as Head of Richmond School, Yorkshire, he had increased its numbers from 15 to 150. Only at Reading School where he went next had he had trouble, but he was so sure that he had been in the right in his disagreement with the trustees that he included with his testimonials several press reports of his resignation. The testimonials themselves came from the Lord Chancellor, two bishops, four heads of Oxford colleges, two heads of well known public schools, and 20 other important gentlemen.

To the boys he soon became known simply as The Doctor. 'He was handsome, stately with an exquisite deep bass voice like sable velvet,' according to Edwin Clark (1887–93), and 'inspired much unnecessary awe'.

King's was at a high point in its fortunes, with more boys than ever before, and for several years it continued to prosper. In October 1882 Stokoe wrote to the Council about the year's Oxford and Cambridge Board results. 'The tabulated statement in the *Guardian*, which I send with this, is the best way of showing how we stand. Eton, who sent in at least 60 candidates, gained 31 certificates. We, with 41 candidates, gained 30 … Marlborough came next to us with 23 – no other school has over 20.' To Oxford and Cambridge universities the School had gained more open awards 'than in any recent year'.

In non-academic ways the School also continued to prosper. At last it had a Cricket Club, even if its ground was far away at Wormwood Scrubs. 'To get to the Scrubbs,' James Everidge (1895–7) remembered, 'we had to travel by Underground Railway from the Temple station. The trains were then powered by steam locomotives and there was little ventilation. Yellow sulphurous smoke filled the tunnels and got into the back of our throats.' Everidge remembered other disadvantages. 'Adjoining our cricket field was the Gun Club, where live pigeon shoots were held frequently. The pigeons were ejected from traps and the sight of these unfortunate creatures being killed or wounded offended my sense of fairness ... My day was spoilt if a half-blinded or wounded bird flopped down at my feet during a game. Unsatisfactory the Scrubs ground may have been, but it was better than none, and in 1883 Stokoe persuaded the Council to finance its hiring by adding five shillings a year to the fees.

By 1880 a Debating Club existed (its surviving minute-book No. 3 starts on 18 February) and in October that year it formally separated itself from the Literary Union, the members of which 'having almost ceased to take an interest in the debates'. 'All theological subjects are excluded,' Rule 14 ordered. Rule 18 allowed the committee to elect Old Boys as honorary members, and it was from the Debating Club's annual dinners that the Old Boys' Club now developed. In 1883 Sir William Christie (1860–4, the Astronomer Royal) was described as Chairman. In July 1884 Old Boys were sent a circular inviting them to join an Old Boys' Club, and by 1 December a book of rules and list of original members had been published.

Meanwhile in 1883 the School had again won 30 Oxford and Cambridge Board certificates. 'The subjects in which the boys passed,' Stokoe told the Council, 'and the distinctions which they gained gave proof of effective teaching and of industry in almost every branch of such work.' Certainly the breadth of the education which King's offered was exceptional. Stokoe had established a special electrical-engineering class, and for many years boys, for a small extra fee, had been able to attend courses at the College in its medical and architectural departments, this accounting for the number of architects and medical men it produced.

But already in 1883 there was a worrying sign of what was to come. Despite the certificates gained there were 80 fewer boys in the School than two years before. The following May Stokoe wrote to the Council to say that he expected the decline to become serious. The cause, he explained, was the City of London School's move to fine new premises on the Embankment, and St Paul's move to Hammersmith, where it had extensive playing fields and could provide the sporting activities which parents now considered a vital part of public school education. Stokoe was proved right. While numbers at St Paul's rose to 500 (from 150 in the 1860s), and the City of London School trebled its intake within three years of its move, King's by 1885 had contracted from 638 to 513.

At this moment, with the School already tilting into decline, there occurred the most damaging scandal in its history. By now the British middle classes, though increasingly addicted to public schools, were also increasingly anxious about brutality at these. Twelve years earlier there had occurred at Winchester the 'Great Tunding Scandal', when a prefect gave a 17-year-old boy 30 blows across the back, breaking five ground-ash sticks in the process. *Tom Brown's Schooldays*, published in 1857 as a tribute to Dr Arnold, was beginning to seem more memorable for Flashman's roasting of Tom Brown.

Now, on the evening of Friday, 10 April 1885, Charles Bourdas, a 12-year-old boy in his first term at King's, returned home feeling weak and unwell, and complaining of pain in his legs. Next day he became sick and his father had to carry him up to bed, but only when he promised not to tell Stokoe would the boy say what had happened. 'On leaving the dining-hall on Friday about a dozen big boys belonging to the upper form … arranged themselves along the corridor, and as each small boy passed they administered a blow on the back.' Bourdas added that he had had 'quite a dozen blows' and claimed that it had happened twice before. On 19 April he died.

During the following weeks the Council's reactions to this event were inept even by its own standards. It was informed at once by Stokoe of what had happened, but agreed with him that no inquiry could be started because the boys were on holiday. Stokoe alone attended the inquest on 22 April.

Unfortunately the report of this was seen at the Home Office and the Home Secretary sent a letter to the Council which it received on 28 April, asking what it proposed to do. The Council replied that it was meeting on 1 May and would inform the Home Secretary of its intentions. This it failed to do (on 1 May it in fact again decided to do nothing until the holiday ended) with the result that the Home Secretary wrote again, a letter which it received on the morning of 4 May, informing it that he had put the matter into the hands of the Public Prosecutor.

At last thoroughly alarmed, the Council's Secretary sent a reply by messenger which read:

> The Council of this College have desired me to notify you that the boys of their School will reassemble after the Easter holidays on Wednesday next and that the fullest enquiry will be at once instituted into the facts of the incident which appears to have led to the death of C. F. Bourdas...
>
> Meantime the Council have issued new instructions to the Masters of the School with the view of providing additional precautions against the possibility of any such misfortune in the future.

This letter arrived at 1.10 p.m. on 4 May, too late for the Home Secretary to read it before he gave a highly critical answer to a question about the affair in the House of Commons.

> I think parents and masters are greatly responsible [he said] for allowing the state of things, which is not peculiar to this school, to go on (Cheers). A system of terrorism exists, of which we have an example in the case of this poor boy. He did not venture to tell what had happened, and when it comes to the knowledge of the parents they are afraid that if they make a complaint the boy will suffer; and the masters of the school allow these things to go on for fear of mischief happening to the school … By this system of terrorism … immunity is secured to those brutal tyrants who exercise those cruelties.

Lengthy letters were now published by *The Times*, in which the Council tried to justify itself, and the Home Office explained that, even if it had received the

Council's letter of 4 May in better time, the Home Secretary would not have altered his statement. Among them was one from the head boy:

> Although I do not wish in any way to make light of the recent sad occurrence at King's College School, I do wish, as captain of the School, to enter a protest against the absurd statements which have since been published as to the prevalence of bullying in the institution. It has been stated that it is the 'daily habit' of the 'big boys' (in some cases 'the upper forms') to stand at the top of the steps leading to the dining hall and to 'beat each little boy as he comes out as hard as they can with their fists'…
>
> Now, sir, speaking from experience gained in eight years and a half spent at this school, I wish entirely to deny the charges of systematic and malicious bullying so freely cast in our teeth. I have, indeed, never personally known a case at all resembling the recent occurrence, and to say that such bullying is the common practice of any boys in the school is not the truth.
>
> Moreover, on this particular occasion it was not the 'big boys', much less the upper [presumably the Sixth] 'form', who were in fault, but boys of 14 or 15 in the lower part of the school, who considered this a good form of amusement, and had as little really malicious intent as the most virtuous of our detractors.

Circumstantial as this sounds, there probably were phases of bullying at the School. Edward Wakefield (1860–1) said there was 'plenty at play-hours'. He remembered how he had 'thrashed a big hulking fellow whom I caught tormenting a puny-looking youngster of Jewish appearance, who turned out to be a son of Baron Rothschild'. The two became close friends. And Chalk remembered 'a most painstaking effort to roast a boy in half an hour; it was due not to cruelty, but the careful reading of School novels'. He added that no great harm was done.

Gradually the Bourdas affair died down, and no bullies were ever prosecuted or even identified, but the damage it did to the School's reputation contributed to the halving of numbers during the following four years. So, at least, Stokoe believed. In his report to the Council for 1885 he said that the greatest reduction had been in the Junior School, which now had 'little more than 40 boys as against 80 or 90 a year or two ago … the very small entry of young boys both last term and this is, I fear, to be ascribed in part to the attacks lately made upon the School, which … have without doubt affected us, and will for a time affect us injuriously.'

Otherwise he could only repeat, as he did regularly during his remaining years, that the decline was due to 'the greater advantage and attraction now offered by other London Public Schools, especially the removal of St Paul's to West Kensington, and to the large Preparatory School started in connection with this'.

Stokoe did not sit back and watch the approaching disaster, but made various attempts to increase the appeal of the School. He asked the Council to re-establish entrance scholarships (abolished as unnecessary by Maclear), but only persuaded it to offer three. He had already started a special class in science for potential scientists or doctors, and other classes for those aiming at the Indian Civil Service, Woolwich, Sandhurst, or careers in commerce. In late 1887, when numbers had fallen to 307, he established a complete Commercial Division alongside the School's Classics, Modern and Lower Divisions, intended specifically to prepare boys for mercantile life or for clerkships in the Home Civil Service. As well as commercial arithmetic and book-keeping, boys would be taught French, Spanish, German and Italian, including commercial letterwriting in these languages. During the next four years an average of 80 or 90 boys enrolled in the Commercial Division, but total numbers at the School did not increase.

Meanwhile the Council tried to solve its financial problems by imposing petty economies: reducing the value of school prizes, and the number of masters required to supervise dinners. Eventually it was forced to take the more realistic measure of sacking or not replacing masters (between 1880 and 1889 the staff was reduced from 25 to 15) and reducing by 3 per cent the salaries of those who remained. In 1880 they complained to the Council about their poor pay. Newly appointed masters were now being offered only £120 a year.

Nevertheless there were loyal and memorable masters, among them Charles Webb, appointed by Stokoe in 1886. He taught the matriculation class in all subjects, excelling, according to John Tallent (1889–90) at French, maths, and English history. He had 'a face resembling a Chinese mandarin including the typical moustache', and a cork leg. It was rumoured among the boys that 'Mrs Webb also had an artificial limb, the pair thus having only two legs between them'. Tallent was once shocked to see Webb entering a Bloomsbury pub and only later discovered that he was an enthusiastic player of billiards.

Tennis at KCS in the 1880s. The two boys are Herbert and Ernest Neal.

It is not surprising that the dwindling School produced fewer well-known Old Boys. James Palmer (1882–3), however, became famous as a painter of race-horses, both in Britain and in the USA; Sir Arthur Preece (1881–4) was knighted for his work as a hydroelectric engineer; in 1930 Admiral of the Fleet, Sir Frederick Field (1884) became First Sea Lord; and Frederick Payn (1883–9) was the fourth Old Boy to play an important part in the development of English lawn tennis. The earliest had been Henry 'Cavendish' Jones (1841–7), not a player but a codifier of its rules. He had first written about then published guides to half a dozen other indoor games before reaching tennis via croquet. The code of rules he drew up for the first Wimbledon championship in 1877 are little changed today. Second came his younger brother Daniel Jones (1843–52), one of the founder members of the All England Tennis Club. When many of the functions of this were usurped by the Lawn Tennis Association, Jones, who became the latter's first secretary, was important in framing its rules.

In contrast to the Jones brothers, George Hillyard (1874–7) was a player and a formidable one, winning the Covered Doubles Championship in 1890, 1891 and 1905. (He also played cricket for Middlesex and Leicestershire.) He was a founder of the Lawn Tennis Association, but still belonged to the All English Tennis Club, becoming its secretary from 1907 to 1925. Payn, like Hillyard, was a player, competing eight times in the Wimbledon men's singles. But it is his books on the game which are more significant. He was violently critical of the 'small and select committee of a private club' which ran English tennis. 'To find a parallel', he wrote, 'for the way in which the affairs of lawn tennis in England have been managed by its official Association it would be necessary to seek it in the realms of *opéra bouffe*.'

For the Easter term of 1889 the School had only 251 boys. Now Stokoe was offered the comfortable living of Lutterworth, and not surprisingly accepted it, writing to the Council on 5 April to offer his resignation at the end of the summer term. He added:

> I shall leave King's College with many regrets – the chief of them being that the numbers of the School have so diminished, since the London Public Schools have been able to offer such attractions as to make competition for the time hopeless. I can only say that my colleagues and myself have done our utmost to struggle against the difficulties which have caused this depression.

CHAPTER FOUR

With Bourne to Wimbledon

1889–1906

Charles Bourne, chosen out of ten applicants to replace Stokoe, had taught at Marlborough under Dean Bradley and Dean Farrar, then at Bedford County School before becoming Headmaster of Inverness College. At first he hesitated – he was only being offered a salary of £500 plus £1 for every pupil – but agreed to come when guaranteed a minimum of £800 for his first three years. In appointing Bourne, who was not yet in holy orders, the Council was some years ahead of most of the country's public schools. As late as 1903 when Marlborough appointed Frank Fletcher *The Times* described him as 'one lay apple in the clerical dumpling'.

From the start Bourne understood the difficulties he had inherited. When, after a year and a half, he detailed these in his private notebook he pointed out that he had first drawn attention to them at the end of his second term. The 16 he listed varied from the trivial ('The insignificant nature of our Strand entrance') to the fundamental ('all our rivals have during the last ten years vastly improved their school accommodation and equipment while KCS. is as badly housed and as poorly equipped as it was thirty years ago'.)

He concluded,

> I have endeavoured to think out carefully the position of the school and I have throughout always tried to look on the bright side; but I am forced to the conclusion that the existence of the School is very precarious. The public as a whole show clearly that they do not need us, and it would not be felt as a serious loss in the London World if the School was to go out of existence altogether; the only remedy therefore seems to be to go to some place where there is a public which does need the school.

Opposite page: *C. W. Bourne at the northside entrance to the Great Hall, Wimbledon (picture by Banister Fletcher, the architect, 1899).*

Charles William Bourne, Head Master 1889–1906.

During his years at the Strand Bourne managed to solve some of the School's problems. He told his first prize-giving audience (December 1889) that the Council was going to 'remedy what has always been a difficulty … , the badness of our playground'. At a cost of £700 this was levelled with the advice of the Old Boy, Henry Preece.

The following year he persuaded the Council to increase the School's appeal by reducing from eight to seven guineas the termly fees of boys who entered under the age of eleven; in 1892 this reduction was extended to boys under 12. His aim was to establish the School's Lower Division as a rival to the many preparatory schools besides St Paul's, which were being founded, all designed to keep boys until, at 13, they could take the Common Entrance examination to a public school.

The same year Bourne announced that the teaching of science at the School was to be 'very largely increased' and that a master would be appointed 'whose whole time will be available for this work'. In 1893 he persuaded the Council to create 18 entrance exhibitions worth £12 a year. And in 1894, after 60 troglodyte years, the School at last surfaced. 'I have pleasure', he told parents, 'in announcing that the … rooms at present occupied by the Offices, Secretary's Room, Medical Library, etc., are to be converted into classrooms, so that the whole of the north end of the Main Corridor will now be allotted to the School.'

Meanwhile, as in Stokoe's time, life for the boys was surprisingly little affected by the School's decline. In May 1890, by which time the flimsy school magazine of the early 1880s had disappeared, a more substantial one was launched. 'Assuredly, before the world is very much older,' its first editorial forecast, 'we shall regain our old position, great in numbers as well as great in kind.' Reports followed of the Literary Union ('at present in a most flourishing state', again holding fortnightly debates), and of the relaunching of the Rowing Club. There were also poems, an article on the uses and abuses of cribs, and a letter from the commanding officer of the London Rifle Brigade Cadet Corps, asking for the formation of a King's College School company.

Volunteer corps had originally been formed in 1860 when Palmerston, the Prime Minister, had appealed for a volunteer army to protect the country against a French invasion. Many schools at once started corps, and King's College School followed in 1875, but this unit had foundered. Now, with Bourne's encouragement a new unit, to be known as E Company, was formed. Small it may have been (13 members) but Corporal Brown believed that 'what we are deficient as regards numbers, we more than make up in quality'. Its uniform was 'the dark bottle-green of the London Rifle Brigade, the tunic severely plain in pattern without any buttons, it being done up by hidden hooks and eyes'. (Gilbert Szlumper – 1898–1900.)

In these years the Swimming Club was relaunched, the Reading Room re-opened, and the annual sports at Stamford Bridge regularly watched by a large crowd. A Scientific Society was also started, with the demonstration at its first meeting of a 'Brunsviga' calculator. This 'handy little machine', invented by a Mr Ohner of St Petersburg, was worked by mechanical levers that projected through its top and could 'add, subtract, multiply and divide plain figures and decimals almost instantaneously'. While on loan to the School the newly appointed science master, Fred Carrodus, demonstrated it to each of the upper forms.

Fate, however, seemed against the School and the second issue of the revived magazine (February 1897) announced that the school plays and prize giving had been cancelled because of the sudden death of Thomas Green, master of the Commercial Division. He had suffered a heart attack on his way to school for the last day of term. During his 24 years at the School Green had been 'practically for some years a kind of private secretary to Dr Maclear', giving him an insight into the School which he ungrudgingly placed at the service of succeeding Head Masters.

And though for a time Bourne's measures produced a rise in numbers, they fell in the summer of 1893 to 225. In 1891 three masters had been sacked and now three more went. In May that year Bourne wrote to the Council again urging it to take the one measure which might save the School: move it out of central London.

He had already been looking for a suburban site, and suggested one at Westhill, Putney, with 12 acres of ground. Three years later, when numbers had sunk to 169, he wrote more urgently:

> In May, 1893, I laid before the Council a definite proposal to move the School to a site in West Hill, Putney. Putney and Wimbledon have always been the two suburbs that I have considered suitable for the purpose, and I do not think there is much to choose between them …The School in its present position is extremely precarious. There will almost certainly be a fall in numbers next September; and the present rage for athletics makes it practically impossible for us to hold our own against schools which have playground facilities.

At last the Council acted quickly, setting up a Committee of Inquiry which met on 10 July with Bourne in attendance. He described again the Putney house, but five days later he had found a house in Wimbledon. Known as South Hayes, it had just over six acres of land, 'perfectly flat and of a very convenient shape, so that it is excellently adapted for School purposes'.

> I estimate, [he continued] that out of the existing house there could be constructed about fifteen Class-rooms, or in other words, sufficient teaching room for about Three Hundred Boys.
> A great advantage offered by the site and buildings is that the removal could be made without much delay; this would save much of the 'financial leakage' which would be caused if there was a delay while entirely new buildings were being erected.

Though the Council did not at once choose South Hayes, it formed a committee to prepare a scheme for a move to 'the neighbourhood of Wimbledon'. On 28 July this committee resolved that Bourne and Mr Bragington, Director of the College Civil Service Department, should draw up 'a definite balance sheet' to show how the change of site would be financed. Bourne and Bragington met the same day and afterwards Bragington wrote briefly to the College Secretary, 'The scheme looks promising if people can be found to advance money without a guarantee of interest and without being able to get their money back.'

He then went on holiday, leaving Bourne to prepare a new report. By the time Bourne delivered this it was October and for the autumn term that had just begun there were 20 fewer boys. 'Only two courses seem open,' Bourne wrote, 'either to abolish the school, or to remove to Wimbledon.'

Much of the argument which followed concerned the amount the School should continue to pay the College if it moved, and the amount the School's move would save the College by allowing it to use the rooms the School would vacate. Bourne's proposal was that the School should bear all its own administrative expenses, and should pay a fixed contribution of £1,200 a year to the College, 'practically as rent for the name and reputation of King's College ... Mr Bragington points out that the removal of the school would effect a saving on the Waterloo Road premises [which the College was renting] of £830, which saving should be credited to the school in diminution of the above £1,200.'

The cost of the move Bourne now estimated at about £30,000, the main items being £16,000 for the house and grounds, £6,000 for alterations, and £3,000 for 'financial leakage'. He had ceased to believe that this could be raised by an appeal, and proposed instead issuing debentures. If the School's numbers rose to 300, a figure he regularly suggested to be likely at Wimbledon, it would be able to pay the 4 per cent interest which the necessary £30,000-worth would carry.

But the Council again hesitated and it was another two and a half months before its Secretary, Walter Smith, wrote to its Treasurer, W. F. D. Smith, the future Viscount Hambleden, pressing for urgent action. He suggested that the School should move the following Easter, 'without waiting to see the result of the raising of debentures'.

'I write to you,' he concluded, 'as the matter presses if we are to take advantage of the chance of getting rid of the Waterloo Rd premises, and perhaps you could get the Council to have a special meeting and authorize the removal at Easter.'

The Treasurer replied sympathetically, but did not favour a special meeting which might be thinly attended. Surely the house's owners could wait until the Council's scheduled meeting of 15 January? It would help if Bourne could bring to that meeting suggestions for a site in Wimbledon which the School could use temporarily if it could not for the moment find a permanent one.

By the time Bourne reported on 15 January, with typical energy he had investigated four more Wimbledon permanent sites. None of them, he concluded, was suitable, but he had found a small piece of land where temporary buildings could be erected and concluded that the choice was between this and South Hayes. He had seen the owners of South Hayes and been told that an offer of £17,000 would probably be accepted.

He continued:

> It is most important to come to a decision at once for several reasons: for one thing, the School is at present running at a serious loss to the Council, and a further falling-off in numbers is sure to occur, now that the public know we are contemplating removal.

Again, it will be our duty to give all parents of pupils a term's notice of our intention, so that the final decision must be announced in about a week's time.

Again, if our removal to Wimbledon at Easter was announced at once, it would probably be possible to get from Wimbledon many new boys to enter at Easter.

Lastly, we have the refusal of South Hayes only till the 20th instant; if we lose this property there is little hope of getting a site at all.

The Council was finally persuaded. On 8 March the contract with the British Land Company was signed and a deposit of £1,700 paid. On 6 April the balance was paid. The Council was able to settle so promptly because of the rapid take up of the debentures which had been advertised a week after its January meeting. By mid-February £18,600 worth had been sold, including £5,000 to an Old Boy, Algernon Borthwick (1844–7, Lord Glenesk, owner of the *Morning Post*) and the same amount to W. F. D. Smith. Smith later bought another £5,000 worth and gave his full holding to the School when it became independent in 1911.

Meanwhile Bourne wrote to parents,

I beg to announce that the Council of King's College have just completed arrangements for transferring the School to Wimbledon, and have purchased a property known as South Hayes, on a gravel site, facing the Common, and stretching back to the Ridgway ...There is on the selected site a large building, suited to the immediate needs of the School, and capable of easy extension; the School will therefore be transferred there during the Easter holidays.

On 4 March he added, 'As several enquiries have been made in reference to our arrangements for next Term, I wish to say that the School will be in every respect fully equipped for its work at Wimbledon. The laboratories will be fitted

The opening term at Wimbledon, May 1897, before the building of the Great Hall. In the background is South Hayes House.

43

up ready for the beginning of Term, the Gymnasium will be erected, and all the work of the School will be carried on as usual.'

The gymnasium he referred to was a temporary corrugated-iron building which was also to be used as the dining hall. The laboratories were at first created in the house's outbuildings, but during the first term another temporary building was erected for them. He had also found houses in Wimbledon for the two surviving housemasters, Edward Brooksmith and Francis Speed, to acquire. On 14 April the School's material possessions were carried to Wimbledon in a convoy of horsedrawn carts.

The Wimbledon to which the School moved was no rural hamlet, but a fast-growing small town. Between 1891 and 1901 the population of the parish increased from just under 26,000 to almost 42,000. In the School's first term it acquired 38 local new boys, and though this did not make up for the 81 who had left, many because they lived north or east of London, and numbers were down to 181, the town ultimately became an essential source of pupils.

Equally important was the railway, which had first come to Wimbledon in 1838 and now connected it not only with London but with Leatherhead, Tulse Hill, and Richmond. Bourne was well aware that it was vital, and arranged suitable trains from Richmond to Wimbledon, stopping at Kingston. They would be met, he announced, by omnibuses to take the boys to the School – in practice these turned out to be one 'rather shabby wagonette drawn by two weary horses and driven by a rosy-cheeked coachman named "Appy", who often failed to collect his 2d. fares'.

Not all the boys were pleased by the move. Everidge remembered that the new School 'was not much to look at – an untidy Victorian house surrounded by some half finished buildings. I did not like leaving the old place with its traditions in which I had begun to take an interest.' But once the School opened most found their new environment an improvement. 'Our men will no longer be able

'Badly housed and equipped', as the first official inspectors commented in 1907. One of a series of 'temporary' structures built in the early days at Wimbledon, this one finally demolished only in 1965.

The gym at Wimbledon, which also doubled as a dining hall.

to give the excuse … that the [athletics] ground is too far away,' the editor of the magazine wrote. To encourage cricket a professional had been employed and during that first summer term the cricket nets were 'always full'. Lawn tennis was also popular, 'especially between 5 and 6 p.m., when the courts are fully occupied by the energetic ones who have finished their spell of cricket at the nets'.

The School's new playing fields lay between South Hayes house and the Ridgway, an ancient track which probably led to the Thames ford at Kingston. South Hayes itself faced the other way, looking north across the Common. This thousand-acre piece of 'wild and lovely country' had been protected by Act of Parliament in 1871. In the Magazine, 'Wanderer' was soon telling his readers how to enjoy the Common by constructing a dragnet for collecting specimens from the stagnant pond between Kingston Road and Roehampton. He advised keeping it out of sight while carrying it from the School and making sure no keepers were in sight before using it. He also warned about vipers in the long grass near Caesar's Woods. A friend of his had been bitten and 'although remedies were promptly applied, he nearly lost his life'.

The town was a significant new influence in other ways. The Council now received regular complaints about the bad behaviour of boys out of school. In May 1902 its Secretary submitted a memorandum in which he claimed to know parents who had decided not to send their sons to the School for this reason. The Head Master, he continued, had made enquiries and was 'convinced that rumours have been set afloat maliciously, probably by persons who were aggrieved at the School having been removed to Wimbledon'.

Some of these were probably Wimbledon Urban District councillors, and responsible for the Council refusing several times to extend the permitted life of the temporary science building, on the grounds that it infringed fire regulations.

A particular grievance was the effect the School had had on St George's College, a local proprietary school in which they had shares. For more than a year the St George's College affair was one of Bourne's most distracting worries.

It had been founded and run for the previous 25 years by a Mr W. H. Bedbrook, who considered (correctly) that the arrival of King's had ruined him. At first 17, ultimately 40, of his pupils were withdrawn by their parents and sent to King's instead. Bedbrook devised various plans for co-operating with Bourne, their basis that he would run St George's either as a junior school or as a boarding house for King's, but eventually all that the Council offered him was a position as a master at King's with a salary of £135. In response Bedbrook issued a writ against the Council alleging breach of contract, but the court ruled against him and there the affair ended. Though essentially irrelevant, it was an example of Bourne's Wimbledon difficulties, requiring him to write over 50 long and carefully argued letters.

The central problem from which it distracted Bourne's attention was that his forecast of a strong growth in numbers proved hopelessly optimistic. 'If 300, why not 600,' he said at his first Wimbledon Prize Day. Not until 1904 did numbers reach exactly 300, before then varying between 181 and 283.

Banister Fletcher's whole scheme for KCS in 1899. Only the Great Hall was completed.

There were two underlying reasons: the School's primitive premises and its diminished academic reputation. And as ever it was the College's chronic shortage of money which hindered the solving of them. There was, Bourne told the Council, 'a widespread feeling that our present accommodation is of a "makeshift" description, and I know that boys have been lost to us owing to this impression.' But only £23,000 worth of debentures had eventually been sold and by the time South Hayes had been bought and alterations and temporary buildings paid for, less than £2,000 remained.

Nevertheless Bourne now asked the Council for a 'Great Hall', sending a plan of what he wanted, and the Council took the advice of the College's Professor of Architecture, Banister Fletcher. Fletcher proposed a block of six classrooms with a Great Hall above, and though Bourne believed that putting the hall below would be cheaper it was Fletcher's plan which the Council accepted, signing a contract for the classrooms in April 1898. Three months later it agreed to the building of the hall, bringing the total cost to £7,139. To cover this it made a second offer of debentures and took out a mortgage on the School's buildings.

A similar view to that on page 43, taken immediately after the building of the Great Hall in 1899.

By mid-1899 the hall and classrooms had been built and on 6 July they were formally opened by the Duke of Cambridge. For the occasion 1,000 people crowded into the Great Hall. After the singing of 'God Save the Queen', Marjorie Bourne, 'the pretty little daughter of the headmaster ... mounted the steps of the platform and gracefully presented His Royal Highness with a button-hole, which he placed in his coat' (*Surrey Comet*). Inside the hall the 2nd Volunteer Battalion of the East Surrey Regiment provided a guard of honour, and after the speeches, while refreshments were being taken in the School grounds, the Royal Handbell Ringers gave 'a capital performance upon their sweet-toned handbells'.

Bourne organised three further improvements at Wimbledon, one of great importance. In 1898 he appealed for money for two fives courts. About a third of the cost of £154 was donated, the rest raised as a bank overdraft (which it took seven years to repay with profits from the athletic and swimming sports).

Five years later he bought a third temporary building, to be a dining hall instead of the gymnasium. It cost £250 and was erected on the site of the old vinery.

In November of the same year he heard that a piece of land adjoining the School's playing field was to be sold. It was, he told the Council, 'the most important matter ... that has cropped up since we came here, and I sincerely trust a solution can be found'. The School was already renting an additional ground at Cottenham Park, but was liable to lose this at any moment since land there was being sold for building.

Opposite page: Watercolour drawings by pupils of John Sell Cotman at KCS in 1834–5. The lower picture contains puns on the words 'Boxing Day'.

When the Council hesitated because, as usual, it had no money (it had just spent £15,000 on science laboratories and workshops for the College) Bourne launched an appeal for the £10,000 being asked. £1,000 had already been

The interior of the Great Hall in 1899 by Henry William Brewer (KCS 1847), a well-known architectural artist.

promised, he claimed, by such distinguished Old Boys as Leopold de Rothschild, Sir William Preece, the Lord Chief Justice, and the Bishop of St Albans.

The following January he wrote more passionately to the Council. 'The matter is really one of life or death to the School. If we do not get this ground, we shall very soon lose all chance of being a School which has proper appliances for playing games, and then we fall at once into a position inferior to any other competing school. Nowadays such importance is attached to the games of the School, that our good work of an Educational nature would not compensate for an inability to provide games for our boys.'

Bourne's persistence was rewarded, a price of £7,750 for the new land was eventually agreed, and though the appeal only raised £1,277, the rest was provided by a £5,000 mortgage together with a small gift and a small loan from the College. It was named Major Field.

Meanwhile, his attempts to improve the School's once excellent academic reputation were hampered by the measures Stokoe had taken when numbers fell: special classes and a special division for boys wishing to enter commerce or trade. Such boys were seldom academically inclined, and for a time the School even stopped entering candidates for the Oxford and Cambridge Board certificate examination.

Poor teachers contributed to the problem, but the salaries he could offer prevented him from finding better ones. New masters were still only being paid £136 a year, and by 1900 only one of the survivors from earlier times was receiving over £200. Bourne had had his own salary cut to £680. He was so short of money that, when he had to cancel an Old Boys' dinner, he asked the Council for the £9 this had cost him in advertising and postage. The Council as a body refused his request, but the individual members collected £7 15s. for him.

Opposite page: *Pictures by pupils of Cotman.* Top: *Portraits of Edwards, Blake and Hodgson, respectively Second, Fourth and Fifth Masters, by James Townsend.* Bottom: *Watercolour sketch by Michael Cramp.*

For several of the School's masters their poverty led directly or indirectly to disaster. James B. de Vincheles Payen-Payne's case was one of the strangest. Early in 1898 he was fined 40s. at the South-Western Police Court for travelling from Wimbledon to Vauxhall without a ticket. On being asked to show one he had replied 'season', but instead had given the inspector a visiting card with a false address. When Payne's name appeared on the list of fare evaders which the railway company displayed each month at its stations, boys, parents, and masters' wives informed the Council and Payne was forced to resign.

But he continued to trouble the school. First, he set up as a private tutor and attempted to enrol King's boys. Five years later Bourne reported to the Council that he had lost two new pupils because the parents, travelling home from a visit of inspection, had met a man who 'spoke very strongly against the School', and who claimed to have dissuaded other potential parents. He was, of course, Bourne wrote, the master 'who was dismissed for defrauding the Railway; (he has just recently got two years' imprisonment for a repetition of this offence)'.

The case of William Taylor, a master since 1876, was equally troublesome. In 1890 Bourne had had to warn him against leaving his class unattended while he visited the Somerset Arms, the pub in the same row as the School's main entrance. Three years later Bourne deprived Taylor of his scripture classes, in response to a parent's complaint that the way he taught them was 'most irreverent'. Taylor complained to the Council, claiming that Bourne was incompetent and asking that a committee should investigate the discipline and running of the School. In spite of this he wrote to Bourne the following year claiming poverty, and to the Council asking for a £200 loan.

The final crisis came at Wimbledon; Taylor complained that Bourne was preventing him from getting pupils for extra tuition, something on which all masters now depended financially. Bourne replied that the poor results of his class in their mathematical exam were the more likely cause. To this Taylor answered: 'As you seem, by the tone of your letter of today, to be thoroughly dissatisfied with my work at King's College School, I consider it your duty to report me to the Council, my employers.'

Bourne now demoted Taylor to a class in the Lower School, and required him to teach shorthand. Refusing these orders, Taylor wrote to Bourne, 'Your conduct and mismanagement are so remarkable that I must charitably conclude that you are half-mad.' When the Council dismissed him he went to court, claiming £5,000 damages for wrongful dismissal and libel, but his case failed. Like the St George's College affair, the most serious consequence was the effort and worry it caused Bourne.

Sadder were the cases of the two housemasters, Speed and Brooksmith, both appointed in Maclear's time. Both had spent heavily on preparing their Wimbledon houses, but never had enough boarders to repay their investment. Speed had only eight when, in 1898, his health collapsed. Though parents and Old Boys paid for him to go on a long cruise, he did not recover and resigned.

Soon afterwards (1900) Brooksmith, described as 'a traditional type with mutton-chop whiskers through which he used to run his fingers when annoyed or pensive', attempted to kill himself by firing a starting pistol into his mouth – a

The letter from Taylor to Bourne, in which he concludes the Head Master was 'half-mad'. Taylor was subsequently dismissed.

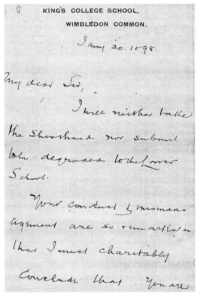

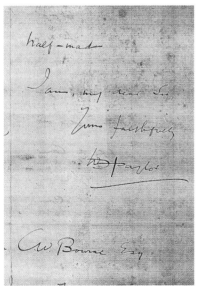

The staff in 1905.

curiously inept procedure for the Senior Mathematics Master. When informed, the Council required Brooksmith to give up his house, which was eventually taken on by Carrodus. Two other masters refused the offer because of the 'dirty and dilapidated condition' to which the Brooksmiths had reduced the house.

A year later Bourne was visited by a sheriff's officer who was trying to recover £45 15*s.* for Brooksmith's coal merchant. The officer was under the impression that Brooksmith was the School's headmaster. Bourne also discovered that Brooksmith owed his butcher £49 at his Wimbledon shop and £50 at his Earls Court shop; and in May 1901 Bourne received a letter from Brooksmith's Wimbledon doctor asking what chance he had of recovering the £762 7*s.* 10*d.* which Brooksmith owed him. Not surprisingly the Council asked Brooksmith to resign.

The careers of two other masters appointed in earlier times, William Larcher (1873) and the French master, Alexandre Dupuis (1875), also ended sadly. When, in 1900, Larcher had been absent from School for 13 weeks during the previous year because of ill-health, the Council offered him a further experimental term with half the teaching load, on half pay. This reduced his salary to £80.

KCS VIB in 1897 showing Brooksmith seated next to Bourne. Brooksmith became bankrupt and later attempted suicide.

'Time was', Larcher wrote to the Council's secretary, 'when a master in King's College School, who had served the Council to the best of his ability for 28 years, would not have been insulted by such a proposal.'

In his final appeal Larcher explained the difficulty which he and other Strand colleagues shared 'when the Institution entered upon a new financial era some years ago, the older members of the School staff were helpless victims of the changes which were then made in our salaries – helpless because we were then ineligible for other appointments by reason of our age.'

The same year Dupuis was also dismissed, because of the 'low state of French teaching in the School'. When he died four years later he was virtually destitute. None of these older masters benefited from the pension scheme which Bourne at last persuaded the Council to introduce in 1901. From then onwards each master contributed 5 per cent of his salary to a pension fund and these sums were matched by the College. French was subsequently better taught by the Old Boy, George Heyer (1881–7, father of the novelist, Georgette), described by Szlumper as the most popular master. 'He was young and good humoured and joined in the games and many of the pranks of the boys, but nevertheless worked a good deal of French into the heads of some of us younger boys.' The French plays Heyer produced for play night (especially Molière's) were so successful that London critics would come. For many years he was Honorary Secretary of the Old Boys' Club.

In its early years at Wimbledon the outside world impinged most dramatically on the School during the Boer War. In 1899 the Relief of Mafeking was celebrated with wild enthusiasm. Twenty boys on bicycles led a procession marching four abreast through Wimbledon, one beating a drum, others waving flags and singing patriotic songs. A dozen times they halted to sing the national anthem, and Bourne made the following Monday a holiday.

School dress, 1899. There was no official uniform at this date.

During the war one patriotic proposal was to turn the School's cadet corps into a King's Regiment, which would include Old Boys and number 700 to 800, but peace came first and on 1 June 1902 Bourne gave another extra day's holiday. Some 50 Old Boys served in South Africa, half as regulars, half as volunteers. One volunteer returned from Canada and was killed at Ladysmith, another brought his horse with him from Buenos Aires. Of the regulars, James Edmonds (1871–9) was the most distinguished, becoming adviser to Kitchener in 1901. In 1914 Edmonds broke down during the retreat from Mons and was transferred to GHQ. When he retired in 1919 as Brigadier-General he was given charge of the writing of the First World War's official history.

In other years the School continued to be busy and, as far as the boys could tell, prosperous. Old societies sometimes failed, but were generally refounded. There was now a Photographic Society, and from 1903 a Chemistry Society as well as a Scientific Society. By 1898 a Tennis Club had been added to the School's sporting clubs; cricket and Rugby matches were played against traditional opponents. All this reflected one of Bourne's central aims: to give the School the accepted features of other public schools of the time. In 1898 compulsory games twice a week were introduced, and an official Rugby football costume described: 'Blue vest with white collar, blue knickers, red stockings with

The KCS Aero Club in 1911, possibly the first school aero club in existence.

two red stripes on the folding tops.' The same year eight school prefects and a senior prefect were appointed. And in February 1899 the Old King's Club, which had foundered and been forced to give up its club room, was relaunched.

The relatively small school of Bourne's time again produced many worthy if few famous Old Boys. However, John Barrymore (1898–9) was a boarder for a year with Brooksmith before returning to America to make his name as a film actor. About his attempts to play Rugby football the Magazine wrote that 'with a better knowledge of the game [he] would have been distinctly good'. Robert Graves (1903–4), aged eight, claimed that his parents removed him because the other boys were teaching him bad language.

Gradually it seemed that Bourne's efforts were proving successful, and when, in the summer of 1904, numbers reached 300 they were higher than they had been since 1887. But during the next two years they again declined, in part as a result of a public recommendation of Kingston Grammar School by the Principal of the College, the Revd Arthur Headlam.

In earlier years Bourne had had moments of pessimism. Writing to the College Secretary in 1901, he admitted that some people believed 'that the constituency that we can conveniently reach is only about large enough to feed a school of 250'. More fundamentally, he thought that King's was bound to suffer, like other day schools, at a time when more and more upper-middle-class parents were choosing boarding schools. 'I am told on good authority,' he wrote, 'that St Paul's is down 60 in numbers.' But Headlam's support for Kingston was an attack of another kind and Bourne wrote to him, 'I can estimate very clearly the conclusions that are being drawn and will be drawn from your intervention on behalf of Kingston; the School is likely to receive the most severe blow it has ever had in my time.'

The incident probably precipitated Bourne's decision to retire, though he may also have doubted whether he had the energy to guide the School through the next revolution in its fortunes: its full separation from the College, inevitable now that the College was to become part of the University of London. In 1898 he had taken holy orders and in May 1906 he told the Council that he had been offered the living of Frating-cum-Thorrington, near Colchester, and would accept it provided they allowed him £150 a year for five years. This the Council agreed to do.

'The Headmaster used to move along the corridors at great speed in a rather crab-like attitude,' Szlumper remembered; 'he had a somewhat nervous manner.' Chalk, however, considered that 'he had the sublime sense to let the good old staff carry on'. He also remembered Bourne's 'sensible grown-up lectures in Christian Evidences to the Upper Sixth. Of twelve members of the Upper Sixth, I believe eight took holy orders.'

More important for the future of the School was Bourne's long struggle with the Council, producing in turn the move to Wimbledon, the Great Hall, and a group of playing fields which at last allowed it to compete with rivals. Few men could have worked so hard to achieve all this, and the years ahead were to confirm its importance.

KCS sports in the 1900s: the West tent-pitching team.

CHAPTER FIVE

Smith Changes his Mind
1906–1910

When Douglas Smith, Bourne's successor was introduced to the School at the 1906 Prize Day he told his audience that he was well aware that the duties which confronted him were formidable. Some years ago he had given up schoolmastering, but he was now convinced that this decision had been 'hasty and ill considered'. Events were to show that Smith was inclined to regret his decisions.

The Council had chosen him with care, first appointing a committee which interviewed 29 candidates, then rejecting the three which it selected and asking it to try again. Of the four it next offered, three were practising teachers, Smith alone an administrator, Secretary of the North Riding Education Authority. Their choice suggests an intention to appoint someone whose principal duty would be to oversee the School's separation from the College.

Smith nevertheless could not escape the problems which Bourne had faced and for these he had no radical solutions. At the end of 1902 Bourne had written to the Secretary of the Council, 'For the past ten or twelve years it has been impossible to get any but mediocre men for vacancies on the staff ... The consequence is that the School possesses few Masters who impress either the parents or boys with the excellence of their teaching.' Soon after Smith arrived he wrote, about a temporary master he had employed, 'I am trying to get Mr F. Draper to stay next term – but he is too good for us at the salary we can offer.'

Before leaving the Strand Bourne had noted in his list of the School's disadvantages, 'Want of an official Preparatory School'. Now Smith wrote to the Council, 'I shall be glad if the Council would authorise me to invite some of those locally interested in the matter to consult with me ... as to the advisability of starting a Preparatory School ... I believe that we ought to start after Christmas

Douglas Rücker Smith, Head Master 1906–10.

An obstacle race in 1908.

The science laboratory in use from 1897 until 1914.

in a separate house, close to KCS.' Christmas came, but no preparatory school, though Smith claimed that a school of this sort would pay for itself within a year.

Bourne noted, 'The fact that we have taken up Commercial Educn. strongly has very probably damaged our prestige in other respects.' Smith agreed. Increasing the teaching of classics, he believed, would 'make for its position as a Public School'. In his first year he made Latin and French compulsory in the Middle and Lower Schools, and introduced science to the Lower School.

In 1907 Smith also invited the first official inspection of the School by the Board of Education. Reporting this to the Council, he said that it had been 'by no means so alarming as many thought possible'. But privately he must have found the inspectors' comments dismaying.

The School, they wrote, needed at least two more classrooms and those it had were many of them ill-lit, ill-decorated and ill-ventilated, while one near the temporary kitchen was invaded during the forenoon by 'distracting odours prophetic of the coming meal'. The desks were old and battered, the masters' common room was 'quite inadequate', there were too few lavatories, and as for the science laboratories, still in the temporary iron building erected in 1897, they were 'so utterly inadequate to the needs of the School that any detailed record of their defects would be superfluous'.

Staff salaries could 'only be described as lamentably inadequate', and the Head Master's in particular (£600 plus free house) was 'altogether inadequate to the dignity and responsibility of his office'. They recommended a minimum starting salary of £150, rising after 15 years for heads of departments to at least £300. 'Only thus can the Governors look to attract ... future Masters', or retain 'the men whose loyal and efficient services have hitherto been so poorly rewarded.'

On the other hand they approved the changes Smith had made to the curriculum which they saw as preventing premature specialisation, and of the dividing of the boys into what were later called houses, according to where they lived: 'Wimbledon', 'East', 'West', and 'Boarders'. Such a division, first reported for the sports of 1907, was logical when competitive team games were so important; soon afterwards Highgate School divided its day boys in exactly the same way.

They assumed optimistically that the School would be free from debt when it became independent (they did not explain how this would come about) but calculated that even so the annual payment of £1,350 in interest from which it would be relieved would barely cover the raising of staff salaries to a proper level.

At the time of the inspection numbers had fallen to 277, and during Smith's four years they continued their downward drift, in 1910 reaching 238. But as in Bourne's time, the School magazine suggested no failure of spirit or decline in out-of-school activities. The magazine itself flourished, in November 1907 selling 170 of the 200 copies printed. In the same issue, however, its new editors explained that their 'task is easier than that of our predecessors, in that all responsibility for the matter which appears in the magazine has been taken out of the Editor's hands. Indeed we find it quite an interesting speculation, guessing at what will and what will not, escape the censorial ink.'

Possibly this was connected with a remarkable spawning the previous year of magazines produced by individual forms, one of them surviving for at least seven issues. They were described as 'not merely frivolous' and one was in French, but the magazine of the Upper Fourth appeared under the title of *Hot Stuff*.

Start of the 100 yards open at KCS, 1908.

57

In 1907 William Treloar became the best-known Old Boy when appointed Lord Mayor of London, and on 28 May he celebrated his elevation by entertaining 'a large and distinguished company' of Old Boys to a banquet in the Egyptian Hall of the Mansion House. Loyal toasts were drunk and the Lord Mayor reminisced about underground life in the Strand.

Sir William Treloar, Lord Mayor of London 1907.

In December that year the Magazine described Haldane's Army reforms. Cadet Corps were to become Officer Training Corps, the aim being to encourage more public school boys to become volunteer officers. 'All military authorities seem agreed that if the scheme does not succeed, conscription in some form or other will be an obvious necessity.' The scheme did succeed and as a result Britain fought two years of the First World War with a volunteer army. In July 1908 King's Cadet Corps duly became an OTC, and Certificate A, which gave exemption from certain exams on the way to a commission, became the main aim of cadets.

Next year Smith announced a new feature of Prize Day; it was to include an exhibition of work done by boys 'in the direction of Photography, Natural History, Construction and the use of Models etc.'. The resulting show was much admired, and on the same occasion the Treasurer of the Council, still the Hon. W. F. D. Smith, announced that £14,000 had been contributed during the year towards reducing the School's debt.

Useful as this was, the debt remained formidable and included a bank overdraft, loans from the College, and a mortgage, besides the remaining debentures. In 1910 these together totalled £25,100. By this time there had been an appeal to City Corporations and the Surrey County Council for money to build new laboratories. The County Council, however, was only prepared to contribute when the bulk of the money had already been raised, and if the School would accept boys from its own schools.

More importantly, on 26 June 1909 the King's College London (Transfer) Act finally received Royal assent. The Act, which made the School fully independent of the College with its own Governing Body, was due to take effect two months later on 1 September, but the Commissioners were empowered to alter this 'appointed day', and did so, postponing it until the same date the following year. It was now that Smith finally despaired, and on 25 September he wrote to the Council offering his resignation.

He had failed, he admitted, to enlarge the School as he had hoped. For the term which had just started the entry had been 'disastrously small': 20 instead of 40, the average in previous years. He offered two explanations. The recent appeals for funds had drawn attention to the School's precarious finances, so spreading 'a distrust in its future when fully separated from the College'. And his own changes to the curriculum. He had now 'come to believe that the policy most likely to succeed is to develop the Modern Side, and its Commercial Adjunct, in such a way as to appeal to the very numerous class of those whose boys are intended for business' – an exact reversal of his earlier policy.

Example of wood carving by a boy at KCS, 1908.

In an amplifying letter he suggested discussions with the Board of Education about the School's future, with a new Head Master. 'So long as I am here the School is identified with my (as I now believe) too conservative policy. Nor do I think that if I stayed … to see any changes through, that I should be effective. It is hard for a man to go back on himself.' In other words Smith now believed that the School's best hope was to obtain state support.

On 18 October, the day before the Council's meeting, he wrote once more to the Secretary. He wished to make it clear that he was not resigning because of ill-health. 'If I saw my way to increase the success of the School with the means at present at our disposal, in a reasonable time, any consideration of health would be of no importance.'

But to the Council it seemed that for Smith to resign, whatever his reason, on the eve of independence would create the worst possible impression and it persuaded him to stay for the Spring and Summer terms of 1910. He then again offered to resign, now admitting that 'my health is a great difficulty'. What was wrong with him is a mystery. He would spend long periods in bed and his trouble may have been psychosomatic, induced by worry about the School. His successor's wife, Mrs Rogers, was amazed to find at first that various people, from the School porter ('full of self-importance') to the 'secretary (cum nurse)' would come wandering about her house. They arrived, she discovered, from the masters' common room via a door specially left unlocked, and had been in the habit of taking their troubles to Smith in bed. When he was too ill, Mrs Smith would do her best to answer for him.

Frederick Carrodus, the science master.

Among the masters who loyally supported Smith and kept the School going were the science master, Carrodus, now a housemaster, and George Wotherspoon, master of the classical Upper Sixth since his appointment by Maclear in 1878, from 1906 to 1913 Vice-Master. Joshua Casswell

George Wotherspoon, Vice-Master (picture by Carrodus, 1908).

(1875–1905, later one of the most important Governors) remembered that if anything happened in Wotherspoon's class which he

> considered unseemly he completely ignored it; for instance, on one afternoon before he came we had pushed one of our number under the table and were preventing him from getting out with a barricade of feet. As Wothers passed on his way to his desk the internee emerged at his feet. Wothers took no notice of him, but carefully stepped over the obstacle and proceeded on his way.

To an earlier generation Wotherspoon had always been 'George', 'but the familiarity by no means indicated contempt but was rather bred of affection ... The Greek play at Speech night was always produced by him and always contained some topical lines added by himself, and so it was that there arose an annual custom: that, when the play was over, he was made to appear before the curtain in answer to calls of "Author".'

Smith himself was well liked by the boys. One of them remembered him as 'a very wonderful man and he had a very great influence on us all inasmuch as he was a gentleman born. I shall never forget that he ran a Confirmation class on Sundays at about 5 o'clock in the afternoon and I am quite sure that he had a tremendous influence on us with his innate goodness and gentleness, particularly as we were rather a lot of irreverent young devils.' The School's Science Journal, with obvious sincerity, commented that Smith, during his four years, had 'endeared himself so completely to masters and boys alike, that his departure will be a real personal loss to every one of us'.

The Council accepted Smith's second offer to resign, but again postponed the 'appointed day', this time to 1 January 1911.

CHAPTER SIX

Rogers to the Rescue

1910–1934

Herbert Lionel Rogers, Smith's successor, was also a classicist – he had taught the classical Sixth Forms at Lancing and Radley – but there the similarity ended. He was a man of greater determination, greater persistence, and above all greater willingness to face the School's problems, a willingness shown when he accepted a lower salary than he had been receiving at Radley.

He arrived for the autumn term of 1910, the last before independence, when the School's difficulties were greater than ever, since its independent survival seemed still more doubtful to potential parents. From the previous term only 204 boys remained. With 31 new boys and five more at half-term this made 240.

Herbert Lionel Rogers, Head Master 1910-34 (picture from 1910).

But already the Act of 1909 had done something to break the log jam – poverty, therefore poor buildings and staff, therefore fewer boys and greater poverty – by laying down that the new Governing Body should include local members. The Bishop of Southwark was an ex-officio Governor, and Surrey County Council and Wimbledon Borough Council were to nominate one each. Other Wimbledon members in practice included the vicar of the parish, a local lawyer, G. Edwardes-Jones, and soon another, Thomas Raffles Hughes. In May 1912 the Governing Body voted Hughes its chairman, a position he held for 25 years until in 1938 he died at the age of 82.

Two things of equal importance now happened more or less simultaneously. At the Governing Body's second meeting (March 1911) it agreed to appeal to the Wimbledon and Surrey education authorities for financial help. This had been attempted in Smith's time but was only likely to be successful under the transformed Governing Body. Negotiations led to a conference at Caxton Hall in January 1912 and eventually to an agreement that King's should receive an annual grant, starting with £500, on condition that it took up to 10 per cent of its new boys from the county's elementary schools. The first three state schoolboys arrived the following year. They and their successors were chosen by competitive examination, and for over 30 years were of the greatest importance in raising the School's academic standards.

The arrangement made King's a grant-aided school, but not a direct-grant school – direct grant schools had to take 25 per cent from state schools. Nevertheless it gave the County Education Board much power, and from now onwards the School's Governing Body required its approval for all major decisions. It might seem that as a result the School had merely substituted one remote master for another, but there was a vital difference: its new master gave money instead of taking it, and gave it in a sufficiently assured way that banks would lend to the School. By March 1914 it had been allowed an overdraft of £6,000.

Now at last the temporary science laboratories could be replaced. To design new ones the Governing Body chose the Old Boy, Arthur Stratton (1887–8), a little-known reader in architecture at University College, London. Building began early in 1913, but was delayed by strikes and by the discovery that the site was 'water-logged two feet down'. Though Stratton told the Governing Body in October that all should be ready in 14 days, it postponed the official opening until the following term, when this was performed by the distinguished Cambridge scientist, J. J. Thompson. The building was a worthy one, not only adequate for the time but still in use in 1995. Water, however, remained a problem. That March it rose through the wood-block floor of its art room, and continued to do so periodically until new drains were laid.

To Rogers the new laboratories were especially important because of a rumour that he had reduced the teaching of science. At his first Prize Day he emphatically denied this. The exhibition of the School's Science Societies, he said, had been arranged before he heard the rumour, and the School had a science journal which

The Physics laboratory in 1914.

was 'unrivalled in any English school'. The last claim was a fair one. By 1911 the Science Journal, presided over by Carrodus, had become one of the School's most impressive features, rivalling the School's official Magazine, today of even greater interest. Its articles covered every kind of scientific subject, from 'the Telephos', a device for igniting gas lamps by a switch at the door, to 'The adulteration of food-stuffs'. By 1908 it was describing 'The progress of aerial navigation'; in 1909 it had an aeronautics editor, and the same year it sent a correspondent to Brooklands 'in the hope of seeing M. Paulhan do "great things" in his aeroplane'; and it regularly included photographs of early flying-machines. In 1910 it published correspondence between its editor, Leslie Reid (1901–10), and Captain Scott, which had resulted in the School subscribing £9 to the British Antarctic Expedition.

Meanwhile Rogers had set in motion the second and even more important development by at last persuading the Governing Body to take seriously the starting of a preparatory school. When he introduced the subject as part of his report to the new Governors at their first meeting they asked him to prepare a feasibility study. Like the science laboratories, the Junior School was some time in gestation, but eventually opened for the autumn term of 1912. 'We arrived in September,' the Magazine's Junior School correspondent wrote, 'to find ourselves possessed of a big front door, all our own; of a staircase which leads nowhere, save to our own class-rooms; of partitions and doors to shut us off from an older and more wicked world.' The Junior School's classrooms formed the east wing of the original South Hayes house.

'We soon learnt that many old friends had left us, just because they were old, and that, including 18 new boys, there were 71 of us, ranging in age from a tender 7 to a hardened 13.' As these figures show, Rogers had transferred to the Junior School all his younger boys, and it had attracted comparatively few new boys, who might anyway have come to the School. Only when boys from the Junior School began to transfer in a steady stream to the Senior would total numbers start to rise.

As Head Master of the new Junior School Rogers appointed a friend from Radley, Bernard Wood-Hill, a man who was to be almost as important to the School as Rogers himself. Throughout his time – he stayed until 1938 – he and Rogers worked in complete harmony. It was the view of both of them that the Junior School should be an essential part of King's but a separate part. Wood-Hill was obsessive about this separation and anxious whenever his boys came into contact with their seniors, as they did, for example, when they formed a separate queue in the tuck shop.

A boy of 1919 remembered his promotion from one school to the other.

A conspicuously new cap adorns your head as you march proudly to School on the first day of the new term. As you near the School your confidence deserts you and you hurriedly look about for someone you know ... in secret you follow the lead of your own special friend, who in turn tries to follow you ...

That familiar stentorian voice, frequently heard in the Junior School corridors ... is now a thing of the past. How strange it seems that instead of

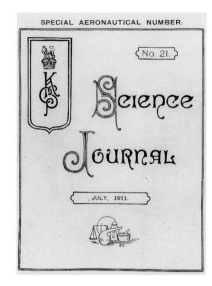

Cover design of the Science Journal of 1911.

Bernard Wood-Hill , 1912.

presenting football excuses to a master, these have now to be handed to a Captain, who considers a cold in the head a poor excuse

The Junior School, one of Wood-Hill's masters wrote, was 'wife and baby to him'. His boys indeed called him Pa Wood-Hill, and he treated them like a Victorian father. In 1914 he was given permission to cane them. Moral exhortation was his other approach, together with rigid enforcement of the uniform he had devised for them: grey shorts, bright red blazers, and bright red caps, making them easily identifiable if they strayed. Donald Jarvis (1923–8) remembered that

> good manners and behaviour were the most important subjects covered by the inflexible standards of the J.S., but minor clothes irregularities were also included. As a small boy I could never quite understand why the makers of boys' cricket shirts … invariably made them with long sleeves and buttoned cuffs, whereas in the J.S. it was a heinous offence to go onto the playing field without rolling up your sleeves.

He was a 'strange almost uncanny figure', Kenneth Cant (1923–9) remembered, 'with a peculiar type of sarcasm. Yet every now and then he became human and toothily smiled at a joke.

'A fair proportion of boys used to have milk given out by masters at break in the hallway of the J.S. It always seemed odd to see B. W-H dishing out milk in an awed silence, broken by "You bowled very well yesterday, no wickets, but you bowled well".'

To Peter Gerhold (1928–34) Wood-Hill was 'a beast but a just beast', who seemed to have stepped straight out of a Victorian school story.

Rogers's annual Prize Day speeches catch the flavour of his early years. He was not afraid to speak sternly to the people of Wimbledon who, he told them, should no longer look on the School 'as an alien in their midst, to be watched and criticised, but rather as one of their chief assets'. Mostly, however, he spoke again and again of the School's merits. It would in course of time, he believed, 'become the most important of the first-grade schools in the South-Western district of London'. Its grounds were 'an unparalleled possession – which might well be envied by any London school'. He had been struck

> with the liveliness and vigour of this place. Indeed, he sometimes thought they ran the risk of the opposite danger of dissipation of energies, for there existed so many institutions outside the ordinary work and recreation that the senior boys had claims made upon their activities such as could be met nowhere else … yet the cry was always for more.

It was a cry in which Rogers himself joined. Among the new activities he promoted was a museum, of which Carrodus took charge. By December 1912 it contained, besides butterflies, birds' eggs, arrow heads, coins, and skulls, 'an autographed letter of the late President Kruger' and 'a patent granted to one Thomas Blundell, for an improvement to chimneys'.

Rogers was also the president of a school mission which King's in 1913, somewhat tardily, followed other schools in establishing. It first functioned in a poor

Opposite page: *Rushmere, the new Junior School.*

part of South Wimbledon where it started a Boys Club, then moved to the Parish Hall in Herbert Road, where

> instead of numbers of boys wandering aimlessly about, … unable or disinclined to settle down to any one form of amusement, we now have many more applications for the use of the billiard-table than we can possibly entertain … Similarly the Ping-Pong tables are in continuous use … while the gymnastic class on Wednesdays … has met with greater success than we had dared to hope. Boxing, again, is thoroughly enjoyed, while chess, draughts, etc., and the reading-room provide welcome relaxation.

By 1913 a Music Society had been formed and Rogers thanked Percy Bull for starting 'Nine o'clock Concerts'. The same year he appointed C. F. Rhead, son of a Royal Academician, to take charge of art. He even wrote a school song, starting:

> To the roof that rises o'er us
> Lift the name we raise in chorus
> High as others have before us:
> King's for ever! King's!

and had it printed on a card to be given to new boys. First set to the tune of 'Men of Harlech', Basil Harwood composed a new one for it in 1920, and it was still being sung in the early 1950s.

In these pre-war years a much needed pavilion between the cricket and Rugby fields, designed to face both ways, was built, its cost (£470) raised by subscription. More significantly, in 1913 the two private boarding houses were closed and as a substitute the School rented Carrodus's house, Glencairn, appointing him its first housemaster; in effect this ended any tendency the School might have had to turn itself into a boarding school.

Opposite page: *South Hayes, 1994.*

The Pavilion, built 1914. Designed by George Arthur Lansdown FRIBA, an Old Boy, who presented the design to the School.

Most original, but saddest of Rogers's innovations, was a succession of German visits – the first exchanges of this sort made by any British school. They began in the Easter holidays of 1911 when the German master, F. W. Koch, took 15 boys to his old school of Godesberg in the Rhineland. 'At Godesberg,' Rogers said in his 1911 Prize Day speech, 'everything was done to help forward and perfect the school. From the Burgomaster downwards all were willing to make its course plain sailing, and to relieve it of its burdens' – remarks undoubtedly aimed at the people of Wimbledon, but which showed a genuine admiration for the way Germany supported its schools. 'If the boys of our Empire learn to know the countries, institutions and ways of foreign nations,' he added, 'then we would be less likely to be engaged in ignorant and senseless struggles.'

In Germany the King's boys attended classes at the school (where they found school hours – 8 a.m. to 1 p.m. – 'a great improvement on ours'), went sightseeing in Cologne, visited a steelworks, climbed mountains and walked and boated on the Rhine. On Easter Sunday they collected eggs in the garden of the Rector (Head). 'This is rather a solemn sort of fun, consisting of hunting about bushes and holes in the garden for coloured hard-boiled eggs.'

The following 27 May, 17 German boys from Godesberg arrived at Wimbledon, where they spent mornings attending classes. They envied the School's playing fields. ('Ah! if only we could have such grounds in Godesberg, then were our school perfect.') When a cricket match was staged they 'followed the course of the game, which was quite new to us, with great interest'. They also watched the drilling of the OTC and 'regretted not having a similar thing in our school'. And they made an even more ambitious series of expeditions, one of them to the Lyceum to see the King's Old Boy, Martin Harvey (1868), playing his famous role as Sidney Carton in an adaptation of *Tale of Two Cities*. Rogers himself took them to Oxford and in a farewell speech said he hoped that when he visited Godesberg he would be received not as a stranger but as a friend.

In 1911–12 there was an exchange of boys for a whole year. One of the German boys to come to King's was Richard-Walther Darre, later to become Hitler's Agriculture Minister and be sentenced at Nuremberg to five years' imprisonment. At King's he boarded with Carrodus who, he claimed, first interested him in eugenics.

In the Easter holidays of 1914 Rogers went to Germany, and returned with another idea. German schools would commonly have a botanical garden and he was now arranging one for King's. A patch of ground behind the library was walled off, an artificial pond and rockery created, and beds dug for the 'frequent consignments of plants' sent by Mr Dulake (probably the father of two boys in the school) from his Brighton nursery. It was hoped that a society would be formed for 'the furtherance of botanical knowledge among the members (many of whom are somewhat hazy on the subject)'.

Rogers's speeches undoubtedly created new confidence in the School, but they hid matters which were unsatisfactory, one of them his relationship with the boys: they did not like him. The stern discipline he imposed was a disagreeable contrast to Smith's relaxed regime. He probably had no alternative. Mrs Rogers remembered that 'the rebellious behaviour in the top of the school … had a slightly vicious flavour' and 'was caused by the fact that gambling etc. was common in the 6th form'. On one occasion, according to legend, a group of boys marched into Wimbledon in protest, but against what has been forgotten.

He was strict with the staff too. Mrs Rogers remembered finding some juniors playing cricket. 'It was chaos!!! No master was visible, only one boy seemed to know the rules … The bat was held on to by two little bullies who invented reasons for staying in. I asked them where their master was and they all replied together "behind the bushes, the bottles", and made signs of going to sleep. At first I thought he must be ill and might need first aid.' When they enlightened her she reported the incident to Rogers and 'the master concerned appeared no more'.

Certainly Rogers was an austere, unbending man. He walked 'fast and with a long stride, his gown usually streaming out behind'. To one boy he seemed 'little more than a gown, a mortarboard and a moustache that should be avoided whenever possible'. Soon he was given a name, 'Bertie'. And though this was affectionate rather than hostile, they came to find his peculiar pronunciation of certain words ludicrous (Kin-e-mar for cinema, be-a-no for beano; the penultimate syllables accentuated as in Italian).

His occasional poems in the School magazine, some with verses in Greek and Latin, gained him respect rather than popularity, and the same was true of his cricketing performances (when almost 50 he scored 71 not out in his final appearance against the School). His interest in the game was genuine, but at School matches he would place his deck chair 'near the rifle range, far away from the Pavilion, where boys and parents gathered'. Frank Freeman (1922–7, captain of cricket) could not 'remember Bertie ever commenting on the success or failure, of me or my team'.

Watching behind the nets one day, Rogers used his umbrella so vigorously to demonstrate a square cut that it snapped. 'Oh bother,' he said (according to one version of the story) and walked away. When Norman Latchford (1922–3) became the first schoolboy to be selected to play tennis at Wimbledon he was summoned by Rogers who said to him 'what is this I read in the paper about you playing in the Wimbledon Championship? They take place during term, don't they? Well, I don't see how I can give you time off, but I will think it over.' It took Rogers four days to decide to allow Latchford to play.

On the other hand successes of school teams gave him great pleasure. When, with many staff and boys, he welcomed the Shooting VIII at Wimbledon station after it had won the Ashburton Shield for the first time in 1932, S. O. B. Powell (1923–30) remembered him standing slightly apart from the others, smiling and visibly moved.

He was no doubt aware of his difficulty in relating to the young, for he began during the war to invite boys, two at a time, to tea. Gordon Walter (1910–19) and his fellow guest agreed afterwards that it was one of the most uncomfortable hours they had ever spent. The teas were abandoned, but some 12 years later he started inviting pairs of boys to dine with him before the Nine o'clock Concerts. One boy would take Mrs Rogers in to dinner, the other his daughter, Renee. Cant remembered one of these dinners as a relatively relaxed affair, even though he did not know what to do with his fingerbowl and peeled his apple into it.

The scoreboard reads:

KING'S COLLEGE SCHOOL 200' 500'

					200'	500'
S. EDWARDS					34	65
C. de LAUNAY					37	56
L/Cpl HOUSDEN					30	58
L/Cpl KERRIDGE					31	61
S. OSWICK					35	66
C. TURVEY					34	64
Cpl LLOYD					29	60
Cpl RILEY					251	493

Celebrations on winning the Ashburton Shield, 1934.

Reserved Rogers may have been, but Arthur Oldham (1919–22) thought that he had 'an instinctive sense of theatre'. Normally he played the Edwardian headmaster, but he was equally at ease playing the stimulating teacher, and many boys remembered his teaching with excitement, especially his French classes. Sometimes he would read a French play, taking all the parts himself 'with ease and great humour'.

His speeches also hid his difficulties with the Governing Body, mostly about its parsimonious management of the School. Almost at once it supported the Board of Education's proposal for an increase in the School's fees by £1 a term, and only with difficulty did he persuade it to exclude boys entering under 12. When it agreed in 1913 that Koch should take an extra master on his third German trip it voted him an extra £5 for the purpose, and at the same time refused J. H. Pullein Thompson £15 to go to Spain 'for the good of his geographical work'. The College did not set a good example. In November 1912 it told the Governors that regretfully it would in future have to charge them for the teas it served when they met there. The Governors replied that they shared the College's regret.

Typically, the Governing Body had only accepted the contractor's tender for the new science laboratories on condition that it was reduced by £600, But in July 1915, when Governor Edwardes-Jones reported that he had got the cost of coal reduced by a shilling to 32s. a ton it ordered 30 tons. In 1913 it told Rogers to write to retired housemaster Brooksmith and retired German master Reinicke, about their allowances, telling them that it must cut expenses for which it was not legally liable. Subsequently it tried to get the College and the Board of Education to pay these allowances, but failed and agreed to continue them, while admitting no legal liability. In 1916 when Brooksmith died it refused an allowance to his widow.

In May 1912 the Governing Body agreed to improve somewhat the basic salaries of staff – £250 for the four heads of departments and £160 for assistant masters, each rising by £10 a year – but these increments were only to be paid 'so far as the finances of the School permit'. They rarely did.

Rogers's endurance reached its limit in 1915 when the Governing Body required his part of South Hayes for other purposes and rented him a new house – Elmdene, on the Ridgway. While he and his family were on holiday one of their maids phoned to say that builders were 'pulling down' some of their rooms.

> We returned in haste [Mrs Rogers continued]. There was no communication from the Governing Body. They had not arranged for Elmdene to be ready for us. In fact it was in disarray! No explanation has ever been given … This was a climax in the endurance of H. L. R[ogers]. As soon as we were fixed up in Elmdene H. L. put in for the first headship which became vacant. He did not get it.

Early in 1911 Rogers and the two masters in charge of the Corps signed an appeal for contributions to the building of a new 25-yard rifle-range in the School grounds. Until then there had been a range in the Great Hall – not apparently considered dangerous, though smelly, and inconvenient: since it meant the Hall was not free for boys to do 'special work' after 4 p.m. £86 was collected – the Hon. W. F. D. Smith as usual making the largest contribution (£10) – and by the summer the range had been built. It had 'no black and white targets', but 'figures of men and horses that can be made to appear and disappear at the pleasure of the officer in charge'. At the opening of the range Lady Esther Smith (wife of W.F.D.) fired the first shot and missed. Luckily her second shot was a hit.

Now the magazine carried an increasing number of reports of the activities of the OTC. Cadets who passed Certificate A were listed and so were the scores at Bisley where the School VIII shot annually in the Ashburton Shield competition. There were frequent field-days, and each summer a detachment of about 50 went to camp near Aldershot or Tidworth.

Rogers supported the Corps. In spite of his admiration for German schooling, he had strong patriotic feelings; when the father of Brian Tebb (1911–15), a doctor and a pacifist, wrote to protest against 'teaching young boys to learn warlike methods', Rogers 'assembled the whole school in the Great Hall and told us that one of the parents had written a disgraceful letter to him'. Fortunately Tebb did not discover until many years later that the letter had come from his father. During the war, indeed, Rogers became violently anti-German, and in the 1920s transferred his admiration to things Italian.

In July 1914 the Corps went as usual to summer camp, this time at Rugeley in Staffordshire, but as the days passed

> the air thickened with rumours. Battalion commanders themselves were so infected with the general excitement, that they were known to stop operations, while copies of *The Times*, specially sent for by motorcycle dispatch riders, were served out to the company commanders on both sides. Gradually our staff officers were withdrawn, our Army cooks disappeared en masse. Cadets ... nobly stepped into the breach, but finally, two days before the end of camp was due, we were informed that the War Office wanted our tents, our mackintosh sheets, our blankets, and home we were packed. The next day war was declared.

At first the most serious effect on the School was the disappearance of its young masters. H. J. Pullein-Thompson was typical. From 1909, when he arrived, a 6ft. 2in. athlete from Cambridge, until 1914 the Magazine is littered with references to him, either as the inspirer of the School's Rugby XV or as 2nd in command, eventually Commander, of the Corps. The credit for the XV's successful 1911 season was 'due entirely to Mr Hankin and Mr Thompson, whose untiring energy in helping and coaching us has been appreciated by everyone concerned'. That July, on the march to camp, 'After a good rest of some hours an energetic party under Lieut. Thompson volunteered to go in advance to Worplesdon ... and get the camp ready for the rest.' He was chairman of the Games Committee, brought his own cricket eleven annually to play the School, signed the appeal for the new rifle-range and managed the appeal for the new pavilion. As a Special Reserve officer he went to France in 1914 with the British Expeditionary Force and was hit four times, twice seriously in the shoulders, at the battle of the Aisne. In December 1914 the Magazine welcomed him back, hoping he would soon regain the use of his arms. He did, and from 1916 was once more in France. Though he never taught again at King's, in 1918 he lectured the School on his experiences at the second Battle of the Somme.

Missing masters were replaced by elderly ones, and eventually by women, including Miss Vivien Hughes, daughter of the chairman. She was a professional violinist, and a well-read lady, once lecturing the School on Shelley and his companions.

By December 1914 over 400 Old Boys were serving in the forces and already two had died: Geoffrey Pollard (1898–1903) and Bernard Fulcher (1906–10). Pollard, son of the Old Boy and School Governor, Alfred Pollard (1870–7), had been a regular officer in the Royal Field Artillery. Like other letters from the front published in the Magazine, Pollard's are full of schoolboy excitement at the adventure he was having and British understatement of its horrors. On 22 September he wrote:

> I had an amusing interview with 15 German cavalry 20 yards away not long ago. I had my revolver and two unarmed orderlies with me, but I must have

created the impression that I was at least a squadron-commander, for they didn't wait to see. Nor, to tell the truth, did I ... I dodged round the corner of the wood, 'and so home', as Pepys would say. But the surprised faces of both sides must have been very funny to see. Afterwards I had the satisfaction of directing the attack of a handful of infantry against them: and we cleared them out without loss.

And on 28 September to his sister,

This is your jolly old birthday ... Your jolly old birthday has indeed been a jolly day. Listen – a complete bath, butter for the first time in a fortnight, coffee after lunch (first time during the war), white wine for lunch (first time for ten days or more), and a complete change of clothing all in one day ... Last night I commanded a long column of tired men, who couldn't really manage the unusually fast pace we went at, and so you can imagine my job was no light one ... It's an extraordinary mixture of cursing, cajoling, encouraging and uplifting, and is quite an experience.

After fighting without a break for two months, Pollard was killed by a shell on 24 October.

As the war continued the Magazine published list after list of casualties. In December 1916, after the first Battle of the Somme when the sort of volunteer juniors officers which a school like King's produced in such numbers suffered so disastrously, a single list named 26 dead and 35 wounded.

At the School the OTC had doubled the number of its drills and parades. Camps continued, and in 1917 a party of 50 spent an additional three weeks helping with the harvest at Penrith. Others cultivated vegetables on part of the Royal Wimbledon Golf Club course, and turned two of the School's four tennis courts into a potato patch.

In November 1914 the School had given places to four Belgian refugee boys. In 1915 a memorial service for the dead was held instead of Speech Day, and no prizes were given, the money being sent instead to the Public School Red Cross Fund. In February 1916 the first air raid drill was held. Seniors took refuge below the Great Hall, juniors in a block of lavatories attached to the front of South Hayes. Here they would thud the doors in imitation of distant bombs, to the alarm of their temporary head, J. J. Fulford, a nervous man (Wood-Hill was in France).

The School was not damaged by the enemy but suffered an accident which, for its historian, could hardly have been more unfortunate. In 1916 Rogers had given the Old King's Club a room in the west turret of South Hayes, in which H. W. (Daddy) Price, a master since 1898, kept the School's as well as the club's records. In 1918 this room and most of its documents were destroyed by a fire. A few which were rescued and handed out as souvenirs to onlookers caused additional embarrassment. When boys obtained them they found them to include confidential reports on certain members of staff with frank comments on their inadequacies. Price took parties of boys to see the damage, charging them a penny each for the Red Cross.

In some ways, however, the School was surprisingly little disrupted by the

Brig.-Gen. James Edward Edmonds, Deputy Chief Engineer and future Official Historian, First World War.

slaughter of its Old Boys taking place a hundred miles away. This was partly because Rogers was determined that it should not be disrupted. There is something strangely routine about his regular reports to the Governors. Time after time the minutes record that the Head Master 'furnished statistics of the number of Old Boys serving in the war and of those killed, wounded and decorated'. Occasionally figures are given, but usually not. Rogers did his best to prevent boys leaving early to join the forces. During one of his French classes a German Zeppelin appeared in his classroom window. When this was pointed out to him he observed, '*Voilà le dirigible*', and continued the lesson.

Meanwhile something had been occurring which was to have a more important long-term effect on the School; at last the Junior School was beginning to provide a significant supply of pupils for the Senior. In October 1915 Rogers told the Governors of a rise in total numbers to 294, in February 1916 to 306. By now the School was also recovering academically. Boys had won two scholarships to Merton College and exhibitions to Worcester and Hertford Colleges. Two had passed into Woolwich and four into Sandhurst.

The increase in numbers brought an improvement to the School's finances. At the start of the war the bank asked it to reduce its overdraft limit to £5,600, but now it did better. In July 1917 it estimated for the first time at Wimbledon that there would be an operating profit in the following year. By March 1919 the general and building overdrafts together had been reduced to £2,852.

Eventually over a thousand Old Boys served in the forces, 162 were killed, 169 wounded, and 312 decorated. Of these last Frederick Sowrey (1906–12) is best remembered. On the night of 23 September 1916 as a fighter pilot he shot down Zeppelin L32 over Billericay, the second to be destroyed in this way. At the School Daddy Price went from classroom to classroom 'his face beaming' as he spread the news. Sowrey, he told the boys, had been known at School as 'Frantic Fred'. Another Old Boy, Viscount Michelham, was offering £1,000 to any airman who destroyed a Zeppelin; Sowrey was also awarded the DSO.

In the early 1920s the School continued to expand, numbers reaching 460 in November 1920. But it still had mortgages, outstanding debentures, and an overdraft, with the result that there was no serious money for the additional buildings it now required. Rogers was compelled to buy, first an ex-army hut for £55, then in 1920 a purpose-built hut for £594, both for the Junior School. A purpose-built but also temporary block of four classrooms for the Senior School was erected in 1921. All were to be paid for from current income.

The memorial library, on the other hand, was to be a permanent building. In 1917 a War Memorial subcommittee of the Governing Body had recommended an appeal for £20,000, to be used either for a library, for more school buildings or for more land for playing fields. Rogers recommended the appeal in the Magazine, but there was little response until he relaunched it after the war.

A more conventional war memorial was also erected, consisting of a circular plinth of stone inscribed with the names of the dead, surmounted by a bronze of a nude athlete holding a laurel wreath of victory. This was unveiled on 21 October 1921 by Sir Cecil Hertslet, Old Boy and Governor, and survived until the 1960s when the bronze was stolen. Abandoned by thieves in a corner of the School

Lieutenant F. Sowrey DSO (right) shot down the second Zeppelin over England. He is shown here with Lieutenant W. Leefe Robinson VC who shot down the first just two weeks earlier.

Unveiling of the 1914–18 war memorial by Sir Cecil Hertslet, a Governor at the school. The statue by C. L. Hartwell ARA was stolen in the 1960s and never recovered.

grounds, it was replaced and secured to the plinth with a steel tube, but stolen again a few weeks later and never recovered.

Lack of money caused another post-war problem; though staff salaries were increased by £10 in 1919 and by £13 in 1920, there was then no general increase for 26 years. When, in 1920, Surrey County Council raised its school salaries to a minimum of £250, Rogers wrote to the Governing Body pointing out that salaries at King's were much smaller, and that it would now be impossible to recruit good masters. He had not even been allowed to replace the Vice-Master, W. J. Clarke, who had died in office in 1918.

Fortunately, in spite of the poor pay, the School retained good masters. C. L. Donaldson, a Rugby player, did for the School's Rugby XV what Pullein-Thompson had done for it before the war. C. H. Dann was a successful house-master and Commander of the OTC. In 1922 Rogers was able to say that he considered King's a happy school. 'Schools were very happy places today,' he added; 'they were almost the only places on earth in which they were making men not money.'

Just the same, for the boys the 1920s were an anxious time, with no certainty that they would find work when they left. In April 1922 the Magazine printed an appeal in heavy type.

'Old Boys can give the School valuable help by sending the Headmaster notice of vacancies they may have for boys of 18 and 19, and by giving preference for these to King's College School boys.' Boys who did find vacancies would leave early. In 1929 the head boy, Ronald Owen, future Director of the Prudential Insurance Co., left during his year of office. As in the war, Rogers deplored early leaving, describing it as 'often false economy'. In 1921 inspectors came for the second time and congratulated the School on 'its greatly improved position'. In their public speeches the Governors and Chairman complimented Rogers on his achievements. It is the more surprising that, from March 1921, he was rarely invited to attend the Governing Body's meetings. Until then he had been at every full meeting, and without doubt joined in its discussions as well as making his reports. Now the Governing Body invariably minuted that it 'directed' or 'instructed' him. In Mrs Rogers's words, the Governors 'treated him as their servant'. Only when he acted temporarily as their secretary (while his brother was ill) did he have the power to sign cheques.

Perhaps the Governing Body did not want him to take part in discussing his own continuous requests for money for buildings, playing fields, or improved salaries. But the underlying cause was undoubtedly Chairman Hughes's dislike of Rogers. As a lawyer, Hughes knew his rights: the statutes required the Governing Body 'generally to manage and superintend the school and its affairs', and only required it to 'consult the Headmaster ... on educational matters'.

Nevertheless Rogers managed to get a surprising amount of what he wanted. Though in May 1922 the Governing Body postponed considering for a year his scheme for four new classrooms for the Senior School (on Hughes's casting vote) it resolved instead to appeal for funds to the people of Wimbledon. Sir Joseph Hood, MP for Wimbledon, took charge of this appeal, and the following year the Finance Committee and Rogers were empowered to use what it raised, not for classrooms but to support a bid for a new playing field. Later that year a 15-acre field was bought, to be known as West Barnes Lane field, at a cost of £6,000.

Raising this amount became such a problem that Rogers ended his Prize Day speech of 1924 by saying that 'his dream of last year about getting the money had turned into a nightmare'. His personal efforts had already included dramatic readings in the Great Hall, and fund-raising dances were also being held there, but now a major new effort was announced as 'King's May Revels'.

These took place on 28, 29, and 30 May 1925, and involved every member of the School and every part of its premises. Proceedings on the first day were opened by Sybil Thorndike, mother of two Junior School boys, who gave recitations from

The King's May Revels to pay for the new playing fields showing the style of fund-raising in the 1920s.

Shakespeare in the Great Hall, aided by her husband, Lewis Casson, and her daughters Mary and Ann. Here, too, folk dances were performed by the Lidell Swedish Dancers. Alvar Lidell (1923–7), a Swede by birth, became one of the best-known BBC announcers, introducing Chamberlain in 1939 when he declared that war had begun. In Classroom No. 1 Munthe's Marionettes performed, their theatre created by Malcolm and Peter Munthe, sons of the author of *The Story of San Michele*, who lived next to the School. Elsewhere parents, staff, and boys ran 21 side shows and 38 stalls. In total after expenses £2,591 was raised, and by July the debt on the new field had been reduced to £1,500.

Meanwhile, Rogers was again asking for more classrooms, and in March 1926 the Governing Body set up a Building Committee to consider 'the inadequacy of the present buildings' and what should be done 'to meet present and future needs'. In June this committee strongly recommended new house rooms, dining hall, and kitchens, and the Governing Body asked Arthur Stratton, architect of the 1914 science laboratories, to prepare plans. Four months later he had done so, including in them new classrooms, house rooms, tower, dining hall, kitchen, and heating chamber, at an approximate cost of £30,000. It took the Board of Education until March 1927 to comment on the scheme, the cost of which, it then wrote, should be substantially reduced, but the general plan was eventually agreed, and a loan obtained from Surrey County Council.

At the same time Rogers was asking for one more building – a new gymnasium – informing the Governors that he already had promises of interest-free loans from parents. Stratton again provided a plan, the Board of Education again asked for modifications, but the gymnasium was built and began to function in 1928.

The opening of the remaining new buildings became the main item in the celebration of the School's 1929 centenary. The Governors at first schemed to get the Prince of Wales for this ceremony or at least persuade 'one of the royalties' to attend, but it was eventually performed on 18 October 1929 by the Archbishop of Canterbury.

In these years the School obtained another important extension to its Wimbledon properties, but exploited it in a more than usually bungling way. To the west of its two playing fields – the original field bought with the house and Major Field, also bought in Bourne's time – lay Woodhayes. In 1930 this house and its large grounds were offered to the School. At first the Governors considered that they could only afford part of the grounds, but when the Old Boy, Sir Jeremiah Colman (1876–8, son of the mustard king), made the School a centenary gift of £7,000 they bought the complete property for £11,000.

They were still undecided about what to do with it. Colman's idea was that the house should become the Junior School, but they favoured making it into a boarding house and building a house in its grounds for the Head Master. Dann, now housemaster of Glencairn, was an enthusiastic supporter of this idea. Plans were drawn and building started before, in May 1931, the Board of Education raised fundamental objections which made the scheme impossible.

Work was stopped so that the Governors could think again. Their next idea was to convert part of Woodhayes into a house for the Head Master and the rest including the magnificent Octagon library either into flats or a sanatorium. The

The Gymnasium (1928).

The Archbishop of Canterbury at the 1929 centenary celebrations opening the new buildings.

first half of this plan was carried out, but the second abandoned, and half the house left unused. Though only 18 boarders were expected in September 1931, Dann was compensated with the chauffeur's cottage in the grounds to use as an annexe.

Subsequently the house was found in 1934 to have dry rot, set alight by a bomb in 1940, turned into staff flats after the war, and eventually sold in 1976 for £150,000, the money being used to build today's music school. Not until 1946 were its old kitchen gardens levelled to make a Junior School playing field.

In March 1930 Rogers offered to resign. The School was running successfully – from 1923 it had been 'full' with over 500 boys. By the following year he would be over 60 and have been Head Master for 20 years. Perhaps he felt that his work at King's was done. Unfortunately, as it turned out, he agreed to the Governors' unanimous request that he should stay.

During 1931 there occurred the country's worst post-war economic crisis, and as one government economy the Board of Education issued Circular 1414. This affected the School in two ways: it cut the Board's grant by about £700, and it required the staff's salaries to be cut by 10 per cent.

When the Governors arranged a meeting to discuss these cuts Rogers wrote to Hughes (28 September) suggesting that 3 October was too soon to discuss something so important. The meeting was postponed to the 10th, and before then one of Rogers's reasons for wanting the delay became clear when he and Wood-Hill wrote to Governors whom they hoped would be sympathetic, urging them to attend. The day before the meeting Hughes wrote to Rogers asking why he had not received such a letter, and a vituperative exchange of letters on this subject continued for the next few weeks alongside more dramatic events.

Before the meeting both Rogers and Wood-Hill had written to Hughes asking not merely to be in attendance in case the Governors called them, but to be present throughout. Hughes refused to agree to this. Rogers also wrote to the Inspector of Schools asking what the Board of Education would do if the School failed to impose the salary cuts. In 'somewhat threatening language' the Inspector replied that it might entirely withdraw its grant.

The day before the meeting Rogers received a letter of protest signed by most of his staff. Its essential point was that the £800 by which the cuts in salaries would exceed the cut in grant would go to the School, not to the Treasury for the benefit of the country. At the meeting Rogers was allowed to put this argument to the Governing Body, but Governor Rupert Howorth proposed the full 10 per cent cut, with remission only in cases of special hardship. Before a vote was taken, however, Governor Lord Ebbisham proposed an adjournment of a week to discover what other schools were doing, and his motion was carried.

Howorth now became the most active organiser of the Governing Body's intention to have the full cut in salaries imposed. He was a senior Civil Servant, a former permanent secretary to the Board of Education. Graeme Cranch (1924–9), himself a Governor from 1949, considered him 'a hard man, unsmiling and always following the Establishment line'. After the war he was 'a habitual stumbling block, always ready to delay matters, to take no risks, to spend no money other than could be quickly recouped. By nature he was dogmatic, always keen to speak first ... and clearly scornful of opposite opinions.' It was 'no wonder he supported Higher Authority ... over the 1931 pay cuts'.

On 11 October Howorth wrote to Ebbisham, warning him against making enquiries about what other schools were doing because it was clear that these would be made with a view to possible joint action of some kind. If, however, he continued, 'you decide to proceed it must be most clearly understood that the responsibility and the probable evil consequences which result, must be borne alone by those members of the Governing Body who have insisted on this step being taken'.

Woodhayes, the Head Master's residence from 1934 to 1960.

Two days later, in answer to a reply from Ebbisham Howorth wrote:

What I do so strongly deprecate is that the time before the next meeting should be devoted to canvassing other similarly circumstanced schools with a view to the possibility of taking some kind of joint action ... I would not alter a single word of my letter to you of the 11th October. Indeed the position has grown worse ... by reason of the organised and dishonest agitation of certain London elementary school teachers and certain of the less responsible elements in the Civil Service ...

The mere notion that we might... consider a course of action which has hitherto been taken only by naval mutineers and a few ignorant clerks and teachers, is as horrible and repulsive to me as I know it must be to you.

The same day (13 October) 30 members of the staff sent Hughes a letter of protest:

Since the meeting of our Governing Body on Saturday last [they wrote] important new facts have arisen. The Grant-aided Schools throughout the Country have expressed their views in a strong memorandum circulated by the Committee of these Schools which are represented on the Headmasters' Conference. These views are identical with what we wrote in our letter to the Head Master, and the Committee presses the necessity of united action.

Hughes had presumably received this letter by the following day, 14 October, when he and Howorth met the assembled masters. On the 15th Howorth wrote to Edwardes-Jones that he and Hughes had 'had a most unpleasant time; the meeting breaking up more or less in disorder'.

The same evening at 8.30 he went to see Wood-Hill. He had expected the meeting to take 20 minutes but it lasted $2\frac{1}{2}$ hours. Only now did Wood-Hill become the first member of the staff to learn the real reason for the Governors' wish to retain the balance of £800 which the salary cut would bring them; it would rescue them from yet another financial mess, caused by what Howorth described as 'the Woodhayes venture'.

In his notes on the meeting Howorth wrote:

It was impossible to conceal the fact that the present position was mainly due to the actions of a majority of the Governors last spring, in insisting against the advice of certain Governors [himself, Hughes and Edwardes-Jones] on the provision of a Head Master's house.

Mr Wood-Hill assured me that the masters would ... be unanimous in withdrawing their opposition if the financial position of the School was frankly and fully put before them.

The two men agreed that this should be done at one or perhaps two further meetings between Governors and masters, and discussed whether Rogers or Wood-Hill should be present. 'I was apprehensive that if he was not present the Head Master might afterwards tell the staff that the Governors had told them a fairy story. Wood-Hill agreed with me that unfortunately the Headmaster was not endowed with a financial sense, and that it was very difficult to get any financial matter across to him.'

They also discussed the lack of contact between the staff and the Governing Body. 'As an example he [Wood-Hill] mentioned he had not been consulted in any way in regard to the plans of the new buildings until the final plans had been approved.

'I said that to me this was very astonishing, because in the Civil Service ... complete liaison with the staff was secured, and after long experience I was absolutely satisfied that it was folly to hide things from those concerned.

'We parted the best of friends,' Howorth concluded, 'after exchanging reminiscences of the Oxford of 30 years ago ... I can conceive of no one better fitted to take up the headship of a great school.'

When the Governors met on 17 October they still did not resolve on the salary cut, but agreed to meet the heads and staff on 28th. Before this meeting Wood-Hill wrote to Hughes:

> I am no longer anxious about the temper of the house that will face you on Wednesday Oct. 28 but I am venturing to make this one suggestion. Could you find a way of suggesting to Councillor Jones that, just for one evening he leave the speaking to other Governors? I have heard his 'set piece' twice and remain unimpressed. It contains the word 'unpatriotic' which would loose wild tongues and sting the staidest to retort. Even if it is impossible to cut out the whole speech, could not a diplomatic blue pencil remove this word?

Perhaps Wood-Hill's letter had an effect, because on 28 October it was Hughes who repeated the Governing Body's supposed reasons for making the full cut. In reply the masters, not apparently converted by anything Wood-Hill had told them, argued that the Board's threatened withdrawal of the whole grant should be met 'if and when it materialised', that cuts at King's would be to salaries already below the Burnham Scale, and that any amount by which the cut in salaries exceeded the cut in grant should be handed to the Government. Again no final decision was taken.

Both Rogers and Wood-Hill now for a second time wrote to the Governing Body protesting at their exclusion from its discussions, but at its meeting of 3 November Hughes maintained, as before, that they were not entitled to attend unless asked to do so. Finally at this meeting the Governing Body imposed the full 10 per cent cut, agreeing only to set up a committee to consider cases of hardship. Before they voted Rogers explained once more the reasons for his dismay. 'The School would be the sufferer, since those masters who could, would leave it for other better positions and their places would be taken by "the leavings", i.e. by men not wanted elsewhere. After the gradual progress of the last 20 years ... he regretted the step backwards it was now proposed to take.'

By the meeting of 12 November the majority of the masters had sent the Governors a memorandum suggesting that all staff should be considered to be cases of hardship, but the Governors rejected this, and Hughes asked the two Head

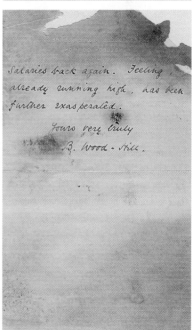

'The poorest of us have to swallow their pride and beg for their own salaries back again.' Letter from Bernard Wood-Hill complaining about the salary cuts of 1931.

Masters to 'help to remove any rankling feeling existing among the masters'. Though Rogers agreed to try to do so, he observed that he 'was not acting in any peculiar way, but that their present opinion was the opinion of the whole profession'. In reply Hughes said that 'so far as the Governors were concerned the matter was now closed'. Closed to the Governors it may have been, but not to the Head Masters and staff, whose bitterness persisted.

In Mrs Rogers's opinion, Hughes's hostility to her husband had begun 20 years earlier at a 1910 meeting of Wimbledon's Shakespeare Reading Society, when Rogers had suggested that it might occasionally read a modern author like Bernard Shaw. 'All were very much on his side except T. H. H[ughes],' she wrote, until 'T.H. made a long speech in an exceedingly rude manner against any change of authors and also spoke of strangers coming to Wimbledon and attempting to change everything.' About Hughes's acolyte, Edwardes-Jones, she was more charitable:

> My feelings about E.J. have completely changed for the better. His real life work was 'economy' even in his own family whom he loved. I was quite touched at his childish pleasure in beating down the King's butcher 1s. per pound in the price of meat for school lunches!!! He put in a lot of his valuable time in doing this. I do like to think of him glorying in the fact that he saved K.C.S. from bankruptcy. Perhaps he did.

In October 1933 Rogers again told the Governors that he intended to retire and this time they did not try to dissuade him, but recorded their gratitude for 23 years of 'splendid service' to the School, which had raised it 'to its present high position'.

Rogers became not just a headmaster but an institution and many boys came to admire and like him. Below his rectitude some now detected a sense of humour. Cant remembered that he would roar with laughter 'at the bawdy bits of Aristophanes! At any modern stories near the bone he would not have been amused.' Others came to recognize his underlying concern for them. Typical of numerous recollections, published on the fiftieth anniversary of his retirement, were those of Leslie Hearnshaw (1921–6, for 27 years Professor of Psychology at Liverpool University). 'He was a tremendous, and to a boy a somewhat awe-inspiring figure. But one came to admire his qualities and his essential fairness and kindness ... His figure was erect and his eagle eyes were piercing. He was completely in control of his classes because he was completely in control of himself.'

CHAPTER SEVEN

Peace, War, and Peace
1934–1960

Hubert John Dixon who succeeded Rogers in 1934 was another classicist: he had taught classics at Fettes and most recently at Dulwich. He remained at King's until 1960, his regime thus spanning a world war as Rogers's had, and lasting even longer. It falls naturally into the pre-war, war, and post-war years.

In some ways the pre-war years were a continuation. The School prospered, numbers remained high (585 by 1938), and a satisfactory proportion of boys continued to pass General Certificate and Higher Certificate examinations – 68 and 18 respectively in 1934, the best result for ten years. In 1938 the School won the two Balliol Domus scholarships for classics, still considered the most prestigious university awards.

Out-of-school activities flourished, now including chess, drama, physical, and wireless societies, from 1936 a German Society and from 1938 a French Society. At its second meeting the German Society voted 13 to 9 that 'France is a better country than Germany'. Boys still cultivated the botanic garden. The School's houses still competed annually in a hobbies competition. In 1934 the juggernaut exhibited by Robert Trier (1932–6) 'was actually induced to show its paces in the School grounds'. The School Magazine appeared regularly three times a year while occasional rivals came and went.

Rugby and cricket teams continued to play traditional opponents like Dulwich, Whitgift, and King's School Canterbury with reasonable success. School events now included an annual cross-country race over the Common. In March 1935 'It was bitterly cold and light snow was falling as the race started ... a fairly strong northerly wind was blowing which helped the runners considerably on the homeward stretch from the Windmill.' In 1934 the Shooting VIII won the Ashburton Shield for the second time, and in 1938 for the third time.

Hubert John Dixon, Head Master 1934–60 (picture from 1959).

Junior schoolboys outside the tuckshop, 1930s.

The Old King's Club now had Rugby, cricket, golf, rifle shooting, and swimming clubs. When Alvar Lidell became an announcer at Broadcasting House the Magazine noted that the King's Old Boys' Rugby Club results began to be 'regularly given in the General News Bulletins of the BBC'.

For leavers it remained hard to get work, and boys who found a job would depart early. In May 1935 Dixon reported to the Governors that although the Junior and Senior Schools were full, the Sixth Forms were not. At Prize Day 1937 he pleaded with parents to leave boys at school until they were at least seventeen and a half. 'A boy's ideas cannot take any shape until he has reached the Sixth Form.'

Meanwhile the School continued to give boys the sort of advice about careers which Rogers had personally given them; and in February 1935 the pre-war master, Pullein-Thompson, returned once more to lecture to parents and boys on the subject. He was now Secretary of the Careers Advisory Committee, himself advising a thousand boys a year. During the depressed years of the 1930s parents had parallel worries; in March 1935 the fees of 17 boys were overdue.

The School's underlying problems also remained the same. These centred on the way it was managed by the Governing Body, and as long as Hughes remained chairman with colleagues like Howorth there was unlikely to be much change. Undoubtedly Hughes was committed to King's. By the time he died in 1938 (four days after attending his last Governing Body meeting) he had been present at 109 of the 124 held in his time. He took a detailed interest in everything that concerned the School – if a drain was blocked he would personally inspect it.

But he gave some staff an impression that his passion was really for managing things rather than for the School. At the first Governing Body meeting after Dixon's arrival the Head Master's attendance was again discussed and it was resolved that it should be 'left to the chairman to decide whether he should attend'. Not once between then and Hughes's death did Dixon attend except when called to read his reports or to discuss special matters. His powers also remained restricted. Before he could expel a boy he was required to report the matter to a subcommittee consisting of the Chairman and two other Governors. The first time it seems certain that Dixon was present for a complete Governing Body meeting was in December 1938, when he offered the School's congratulations to Lord Ebbisham on his appointment as Hughes's successor.

Furthermore, in the opinion of Governor Pollard the Governing Body had not been making proper use of its Finance Committee. In October 1931 at the start of the salaries crisis he wrote to Hughes, 'I am greatly concerned that the Governing Body is summoned to meet on Saturday to consider the financial arrangements consequent on Circular 1414 without … any prior consideration of the subject by the Finance Committee. I think that our troubles earlier this year over Woodhayes were largely due to insufficient use having been made of the Finance Committee.'

Lack of financial foresight led to the missing of two important opportunities. In 1936–7 Redwings (later The Rydons), standing beside the Junior School playground, was for sale and the Governing Body resolved to offer £3,500. A year later it agreed to a total expenditure of £5,400 including alterations, but there the matter ended. In February 1939 Governor Joshua Casswell (1897–1905) told the Governing Body that the Priory, next to the Junior School huts, was for sale and suggested interesting Old Boys in its purchase. In June he raised the matter again, pointing out 'the obvious need for further accommodation for the Junior School', but nothing was done.

The Priory next to the school as it was when purchased in 1949 for the Junior School.

There were, however, changes with Dixon's arrival, most obvious to the boys in the character of their new Head Master. Dixon, according to Frank Miles, suffered:

because his appearance and public address were so radically less impressive than those of Rogers. Dixon had a rather weird vocal mannerism, something like the noise made by a bumblebee trapped in an overturned tumbler, with which he punctuated his public pronouncements, and which were meat and drink to schoolboy mimics. One of these was the comedian, Jimmy Edwards, who used it in his role as the disreputable headmaster in the television comic series *Whack-O!*.

In Miles's opinion Dixon 'lacked a sense of the ridiculous ... For instance during one very hot summer when he allowed boys to be in school without their jackets, he turned up to take morning assembly in his braces, but wearing his gown on top.'

Other changes Dixon himself was responsible for, one of the first being the introduction of 'standard dress'. Prefects and those who had passed School Certificate were exempt, but from September 1935 other boys had to wear black jackets and waistcoats, grey flannel trousers and stiff white collars. They did not apparently object to this compulsory smartening, and Dixon was allowed £10 a term to help parents with the cost in 'necessitous cases'.

His second introduction was universally popular: an open-air swimming-pool. Like standard dress, he proposed it to the Governors during his first report, the site to be West Barnes Lane, and they agreed to an expenditure of £2,000, to be recovered from 'voluntary subscriptions and Tuck Shop profits'. Fortunately it was built at Wimbledon, at a cost of £3,500, of which less than a thousand had been raised by the time Hughes opened it in May 1936. After the speeches the

Standard dress, 1935, as worn by the prefects, with Dixon (centre).

new swimming instructor showed how he planned to teach the crawl. By this time Miss Adair of 104 The Ridgway had complained that the diving-boards were 'very conspicuous from her house', and on 28 May the Governing Body agreed to screen them – too late for she had died on the 26th.

Two years later King's was an early school to introduce a new sort of activity when a Work Team was formed 'to carry out work which is necessary in the School grounds, or about the School, but which might not otherwise be done for some time'. At Highgate Bell (under the influence of Kurt Hahn, the German founder of Gordonstoun) introduced so-called 'pioneers' to do similar work at about the same time, but at Marlborough it was not until the 1950s that Garnett started a Works Group. The King's Work Team dug weeds from the playing-fields, trimmed hedges, rolled pitches, cleaned windows, and levelled ground at Woodhayes for a tennis-court.

There was a change, too, at the Junior School when, at Christmas 1937, Wood-Hill at last retired. At the following Prize Day Dixon said he was lucky in his choice of a successor, but it was the Governing Body which had chosen Venner and Dixon did not consider himself lucky. Venner had been strongly supported by Wood-Hill, who later claimed that he would have refused to resign if he had not got his way.

Wood-Hill and Venner, however, were by no means alike. Clive Hamilton (1955–60) remembered Venner as

> foppish, elderly and effeminate; and at the same time caring and com-municative – particularly of a deep sense of right and wrong. I never in the upper school felt ashamed of my iniquities as I did in front of Mr Venner ... He was also a marvellously adept and funny teacher of French, waving his arms and flapping his gown around, getting us all to chant mnemonics that I still find jolly useful.

Despite the satisfactory state of the School over which Dixon presided in his pre-war years, the staff never warmed to him – as was to become all too clear. 'Dixon harried me constantly,' wrote the most flamboyant of them, Eric Whelpton, known first as Whelpo later as Hippo, on whom it is generally agreed that Dorothy Sayers based her aristocratic detective, Lord Peter Wimsey, 'and, in a sense, quite excusably, for I am untidy and casual and was far from meticulous in such matters as adding up examination marks and writing end of term reports. For my part I am allergic to classical scholars who are not humanists and have no appreciation of the arts. After spending ten or fifteen years in London, Dixon had not even been to the National Gallery.'

The boys, on the other hand, warmed to Whelpton. 'What we got from him,' Ronald Mason (1928–31) remembered, 'was not so much grammar and syntax as sudden and exciting glimpses of cosmopolitan worlds beyond our restricted ken ... in a random, untidy, amusing and very memorable way he opened up imaginative potentialities not only in the world outside but in ourselves.' In 1938 Whelpton and another master took a party from King's on an exchange visit to a German school – ominous resurrection of those pre-First-World-War German exchanges led by Koch.

The OTC annual inspection, 1935.
Dixon is on the right, dressed
in silk hat, morning coat and spats.

On 29 September 1938, by which time Chamberlain had twice failed to agree with Hitler about Czechoslovakia, the Governing Body resolved that if 'the present diplomatic negotiations broke down boarders would be offered accommodation at the Old Rectory, Burford'. The staff, however, were not told of this offer, nor the parents, some of whom were much alarmed by the situation, and a day or two later Venner met a crowd of them waiting outside the School. When he had made his way inside he found Dixon 'who, having hastily ordered the digging of trenches and an educational correspondence course, told me I was to take him to Burford in the Cotswolds to find a house for the Junior School and the Boarding House.' At Burford they found that the house had been reserved for expectant mothers from the East End, and on their return heard of Chamberlain's third meeting with Hitler and arrival home with his notorious piece of paper.

Eleven months later when the war began the idea of leaving London must have occurred again to the Governors, but their minutes record no discussion of the possibility, and the decision to stay, if that is that it was, proved wise. Numbers at schools which went to the country fell dramatically, at University College School by 50 per cent, at Mill Hill by 42 per cent, at the City of London School from 741 to 430, and at Westminster, which went to three different places from 339 to 146. By 1942 King's had only 31 fewer boys than in 1939 (554 instead of 585).

Numbers had, however, fallen at first because some parents had sent their boys abroad or to the country, and in November 1939 Dixon told all staff that

Annual inspection of the OTC, with air-raid shelters under construction in the background.

they should consider themselves on three months' notice. More serious was the evacuation of most of the local preparatory schools, which in normal times provided half the boys for the Senior School. To compensate for their absence the Junior School was expanded beyond its normal limit.

In other ways the School was less immediately affected than it had been in 1914. True, T. G. C. Ward, Commander of the Corps, joined his regiment, but it was only in July 1940 that J. H. Babington joined the RNVR, and Dixon told the Governors that seven other masters were likely to be called up. And though by December 1939 Alan Dilnot (1924–33) had been reported missing (later dead) on a flight over North-West Germany, it was only in July 1940 after the defeat of France and the Dunkirk evacuation that the Magazine reported more Old Boy casualties: four dead and three missing.

There were other contrasts with 1914. In winter the school day was ended an hour before lighting-up time, seriously curtailing the activities of School societies; in the winter of 1940–1 all those which met after school were suspended. And at first boys spent so much time in the School's air-raid shelters that their work was affected. In November 1940, however, a spotting system was introduced, to distinguish between siren alerts and real danger. At night six masters and senior boys stayed at the School, fire-watching in shifts.

Below the surface another drama was developing which eventually surfaced at the Governors' meeting of 13 November 1941, when, according to the final

Dalziel and Dann (left and right), the masters who 'hatched the plot to get rid of Dixon'.

paragraph of the minutes, 'The Headmaster and the Secretary withdrew and the Governors discussed a matter of importance.' This matter was a 'correspondence which had recently passed between the members of the Senior Staff and the Headmaster'. The staff members were probably Dann and 'Duggie' Dalziel. Years later when Dalziel was drinking at the Crooked Billet someone reminded him that he was sitting at 'the same table we sat at in 1940 when you hatched your plan to get rid of Dixon'. Dalziel did not deny it. Both Dann and Dalziel had been at the School in Rogers's time, Dann since 1920, Dalziel since 1927. Dann was now for the second time housemaster of the boarding house and Commander of the Corps, Dalziel was the Supervisor of Games. They had been trusted and consulted by Rogers and felt that this trust had been withdrawn. Dixon, they considered, was behaving towards his staff in a secretive and authoritarian manner, and treating parents with an equal lack of tact by failing to take notice of their complaints or even answer their letters.

Dixon, on the other hand, considered that the masters he had inherited were a poor lot, and was in general unhappy about his job. If he had been told of the School's debts, he said later, he would not have accepted the appointment. The affair is strangely similar to one at Marlborough where in 1946, again just seven years after the departure of a much-admired head, George Turner, senior masters tried to have his successor removed.

At the Governors' next meeting (22 November) first the staff then the Head Master put their cases, and eventually (after five hours) 'the headmaster expressed regret for what had occurred and indicated his desire to meet any reasonable requests of the staff'. The Governors then suggested that Governor Casswell (KCS 1897–1905) should liaise between Head Master and staff in order to help them overcome their differences. Casswell, a successful criminal barrister, was to play a leading part in this and two further King's dramas. He was a committed supporter of the School, and also enjoyed applying his legal mind to the constitutional confusion into which its affairs had subsided – surprisingly considering that Hughes was a KC.

The Governing Body next met on 13 February at Waterloo Station in the office of Governor Gilbert Szlumper, General Manager of the Southern Railway. During the intervening three months Casswell and other Governors had had informal meetings with Dixon and the staff, but failed to make peace between them. At once they now considered the resolution,

> The Governors have examined with anxious consideration the relations between the Headmaster and the Staff. They have sought every means of finding a compromise acceptable to both the Headmaster and Staff, but they have failed to do so. In these circumstances the Governors have come, with great regret, to the conclusion that for the sake of the welfare of the School they have no alternative but to ask the Headmaster to resign.

After all but one Governor had made statements they voted 7 to 6 in favour of the resolution and that day a letter was sent to Dixon asking him to resign.

Dixon did not resign, suggesting instead further discussions direct with the staff, but at these there was again no progress, and the majority of the Governors continued to consider that Dixon must go. Furthermore, on 9 March Casswell told them that it might be less embarrassing if their chairman (Lord Ebbisham) was 'a member of the majority section of the Governing Body'. Ebbisham had not, Casswell pointed out, been re-elected that year, as the statutes required the Chairman to be each year. Ebbisham willingly gave up his position and L. V. Cargill, a Governor for 30 years who had never till then chaired even a sub-committee, was chosen to replace him.

Under its new Chairman the Governing Body summoned Dixon to a special meeting on 14 March. This – the critical meeting – took place at the School and was attended by 17 Governors (though the Bishop of Southwark left before a vote was taken). After Dixon had answered numerous questions he withdrew and the Chairman went to inform him that the meeting was about to vote on the termination of his appointment and ask him if he would resign. When he returned he told the meeting that he 'had been unsuccessful and the Headmaster had made it quite clear that his decision was irrevocable'. The meeting then voted 10 to 6 to compel him to resign, but as the statutes required a two-thirds majority the motion failed.

More committee and private meetings followed, during one of which the Chairman was shown a letter from 16 Senior School masters placing their resignations in the hands of the Governing Body. However, he persuaded them (through their secretary) not to present this letter and now gradually effected a reconciliation. His first step (13 April) was to obtain the agreement of the Governors to a list of seven proposals which were placed in a sealed envelope in the minute-book, not to be opened unless Dixon was dismissed. Most importantly, these proposed the setting up of an educational subcommittee consisting of Professor Halliday (Principal of King's College) and two other Governors (Szlumper was added) which would devise a comprehensive solution to the problem.

Two months passed before, on 13 June, this committee brought its proposals to the Governors. They incorporated several more items from the list in the sealed envelope, including the appointment of a Vice-Master – there had not been one since 1918. About the School's relationship with parents it proposed:

Gilbert Savil Szlumper CBE, General Manager of the Southern Railway, a Governor who was very much involved with the Dixon scandal.

> Complaints from parents to be considered in the first instance by the Head Master and the Vice-Master in consultation. Serious complaints to be notified to the Chairman. Correspondence from parents and others to be properly and promptly dealt with. … In future more consideration must be shown to parents, e.g. in matters such as request for interviews, and for boys' characters, educational advice, etc.

About the Head Master's relations with the staff it proposed that staff meetings with the Head Master and Vice-Master be held at the beginning of each term at which the timetable, all promotions of boys, all appointments of prefects, all prizes and scholarship awards should be made or reviewed. It considered that 'Many of the existing difficulties arise from defects in the present timetable', and recommended that the Head of Mathematics, T. B. W. Spencer, should be made responsible for drawing up the timetable each year.

As interesting as these proposals themselves is the fact that Dixon accepted them; setting a committee over him to make sure he did his job properly was humiliating, to say the least. Obstinacy and a conviction that he was in the right no doubt in part explained his acceptance, but he must also have believed that he was the best man to guide the School to a successful future, a belief which events were to justify.

The Governing Body unanimously accepted the subcommittee's proposals and invited Spencer to become Vice-Master. About Spencer – an Old Harrovian and a Cambridge Wrangler – Whelpton wrote that he was

> rich enough to be able to indulge his fastidious taste in gastronomy and travel. He had achieved great distinction as a pilot in the Air Force and was in every way a modest and charming fellow who was well fitted to be a don at Oxford or Cambridge. I suspect that he came to King's so as to be near London, near his club, and because his best pupils were possessed of a higher degree of intelligence than the vast majority of students at London University.

During the next two years Spencer played a vital peacemaking role. In February 1943 the Governors received letters from both Dixon and Spencer saying that there was complete harmony between them, and that July the Chairman wrote to thank Spencer.

At 1 a.m. in the early morning of 19 February 1944 a stick of 500-lb. bombs straddled the School buildings and playing fields. Dann was fire-watching when he saw the flares, and as housemaster of Glencairn rushed to his house to tell the boys to dress and go to the shelter in the garden. As a result when one of the bombs fell close to Glencairn 'every boy was at his bedside, that is within three feet of the walls, and not a boy was hurt as much as a scratch, though the roof fell in and the tiles and plaster fell over the foot of every bed'. Other bombs

Bomb damage, 1944. Most of the glass in the Great Hall was blown out, the gym required rebuilding, and the Junior School assembly hut totally demolished.

destroyed the Junior School Assembly Hut, damaged the nearby gymnasium, and badly damaged the cottage in the cricket-field.

Though this attack caused the most serious damage till then, the School had already suffered when, in the 1940–1 blitz, fire bombs set alight the Octagon room at Woodhayes. Dixon was away and had failed to leave his keys with anyone, so the fire brigade dowsed the building from the outside, and this was eventually successful. The School grounds had also been frequently spattered with fragments of anti-aircraft shells. Rugby pitches had to be combed for jagged shrapnel fragments before games could be played.

In 1944 Glencairn was re-roofed in time for the summer term, but that July a V1 flying bomb landed on the cricket field. Not only did Glencairn once more lose all its glass, doors, windows, and some interior walls, but much of the rest of the school lost its glass. The Upper Fifth was finishing its School Certificate in the shelter when the bomb landed. Much glass had to be cleared from the dining hall before lunch could be served.

Air attacks apart, life at the School during the later war years continued normally, indeed music thrived as never before, organised by the Junior School master, Keelan Shaw. Typically in November 1940 he and the historian-pianist, H. Greenwood, gave a concert of seventeenth- and eighteenth-century music. 'To end,' the Magazine reported, 'Mr Shaw sang a batch of songs, mixing the victor's joy with the sorrow of the vanquished.' Speaking afterwards, Dixon said that this concert had 'taken our minds off the war with its troubles and worries'. The following winter Shaw revived the Nine o'clock Concerts, with Kathleen Long as a soloist at the first.

Meanwhile, more and more Old Boys were fighting and there were more casualties and honours. Best remembered was Sqn. Ldr. Arthur Scarf (1922–30), awarded the VC for a lone raid on a Japanese base in Thailand, all the other British planes having been destroyed before they could take off. He brought his own plane back to Malaysia and landed it without injuring his crew, but died of his wounds. His portrait painted by Edward Neatby (1900–3) was ceremonially unveiled in the Great Hall in 1947. During the war a total of 1,141 Old Boys served, 144 died and 134 were honoured.

The day on which Germany's North-West Armies surrendered, 5 May 1945, also saw the conclusion of the School's second wartime drama, in which Dixon, far from appearing somewhat unsympathetic, saved the School from its cautious Governing Body. From 1942 the Governors had waited anxiously for the government-commissioned Fleming Report on ways in which public schools could be associated with the state educational system. When this was published in September 1944 they discussed it at a special meeting and were persuaded by Howorth (who had submitted two memoranda in advance) to conclude that 'if it proved impracticable to continue the direct grant system they would, if possible, favour becoming an independent school'. These words obscure the fact that Howorth, as ever the civil servant, favoured direct-grant status and during the next eight months consistently opposed independence.

On 21 October the remaining Governors also abandoned hope of independence after receiving a detailed report from the Finance Committee which concluded that it would be financially impracticable. Though Dixon was present at this meeting and at a further one on 10 December there is no record of his arguing for independence. At the meeting of 30 December, however, he launched an outflanking movement, obtaining permission to 'lay the facts before selected parents and to form a parents' committee with a view to obtaining donations and placing the School on an independent basis'.

A month later (29 January) he reported that he had met the parents' committee, which favoured independence along with the necessary raising of fees to £18 and £16 a term for seniors and juniors respectively. The Governors were not persuaded, resolving on new negotiations with the Surrey County Council, and on postponing a meeting with the parents until the Minister of Education's proposals for direct-grant schools were final. Again they voted that 'independence did not seem financially possible'.

By 17 February they had become 'anxious to meet' the parents' committee. By 14 April, however, they still had not done so and Howorth produced another memorandum, in which he discussed at length the four alternatives: independence, state-maintained, direct-grant, and grant-aided. Now Dixon argued openly for independence, and produced answers to a circular he had sent to parents. No vote was taken, but 'it was clear that the majority of Governors were in favour of independence'.

The decisive meeting took place on 4 May. To this 12 parents came, among them Frank Hole (1919–24), future Chairman of the Governors. Governor Casswell outlined with lawyer's impartiality the cases for and against independence, but also reported the latest count of replies to Dixon's circular. Of the 90 per cent so far received, 86 per cent favoured independence, and only 4 per cent opposed it.

Frank Hole, Chairman of the Governing Body (1950–73).

During the discussion which followed parents were particularly concerned that any sort of grant status would destroy the Junior School by requiring that state entrants should arrive at the age of 11 and be admitted directly to the Senior School. Finally, the meeting voted unanimously that 'This committee is of the opinion that the best interests of the School would be served by becoming independent.' So it was that on the following day, 5 May 1945, the Governing Body resolved by 9 votes to 1 to apply for independence, one Governor abstaining, Howorth the only opponent.

Less than a year later (February 1946) it seemed that the Junior School might after all be decapitated when Dixon proposed to the Governors that boys should move up to the Senior School at 11 plus instead of 13 plus. Though Dixon claimed educational reasons for this suggestion (the reduction of the call-up age meant that boys were leaving the Senior School earlier), it must seem partly to have been aimed at Venner whose appointment he had originally opposed.

The two heads were called before the Governing Body, but 'the exchange of opinions ... made it apparent that an impasse had been reached' and they were told to confer together again. On 5 April Dixon reported that no way out of the impasse had been found. A vigorous discussion followed, in which Howorth characteristically suggested taking the advice of the Ministry of Education, and Venner threatened to resign. The Governors then voted against Dixon's proposal but would review the question the following February. Within two months this became unnecessary when, on 16 May, Dixon reported that he and Venner had compromised on a transfer age of 13.

At that April's meeting the Governors had also agreed to enlarge the Junior School's accommodation to allow it to expand to 280 boys, and discussed an architect's proposals for a new temporary building. In May they were able to discuss a better solution. Since they had failed in 1939 to acquire the Priory, a large house with large garden close to the Junior School, it had been rented by Holloway Brothers as their wartime offices. The School now took on this tenancy with an option to buy at the end of three years, thus acquiring the extra space the Junior School needed. Meanwhile in 1945 a War Memorial Appeal had been launched, and though the Priory was not one of the official objects, it was ultimately bought with part of the money raised.

The War Memorial Appeal provided another example of Dixon's secretiveness. True, he consulted various parents before devising a plan, but when he presented this to a meeting of staff and Old Boys many were dismayed by its modesty and by his having failed to tell them what he planned. According to Cranch, 'the table was thumped, unparliamentary language was used' and 'the meeting broke up in some disorder'. He led the protest himself. A far more ambitious plan was now devised by Casswell, based on an appeal for £60,000, and though only a third of this was raised, it was enough to erect tablets naming the war dead in the Great Hall, support a building programme, and form a fund for educating sons of Old Boys who had served.

The appeal had an important consequence. It provoked Casswell, with the aim of rousing more interest in the School, into persuading the Governing Body to resurrect the moribund Corporation of King's College School. This had been established by the Transfer Act of 1909 and in theory still had more power over the School than any other body. It had originally consisted of the then current members of the College Council (if they wished), anyone who gave the School £100, any Old Boy or parent who gave it £25, and the 12 members of the Governing Body which it, the Corporation, appointed.

It had power to elect these 12 Governors (who constituted half the Governing Body) and to re-elect or replace three of them a year when they retired in rotation. However, it was the Governing Body's responsibility to call meetings of the Corporation and this it had failed to do except when one of its Corporation-elected members resigned or died – indeed, for a number of years the Corporation had not met at all and the annual rotation of the Governors whom it elected had ceased. Consequently, the Corporation had ceased to exercise its other rights and duties, most importantly to receive reports from the Governing Body and to give the Governing Body its opinions on the School's affairs.

By 1947 Casswell was the sole surviving Corporation-elected Governor. Now he negotiated with the Ministry of Education an arrangement by which, in two stages, the Corporation reassumed its right to elect 12 Governors, and the statutes were revised so that they required each such Governor to retire after two years. The significance of the Corporation's revival was that Old Boys (and other supporters) began to join it and so ultimately to acquire control over the School. It held its first Annual General Meeting in December 1947 and at this meeting

Weycroft, the school boarding house, purchased in 1948.

Frank Hole was elected a Governor. Hole was now Chief Assistant to the Manager of the LMS Railway Company, and had much experience in negotiating with staff. Though the most influential he was only one of a number of experienced professionals (including Brigadier A. G. Bonn of Costains, Frank Smith, Vice-Chairman of Warburgs, and K. G. McNeil, Vice-Chairman of Lloyd's) who began to replace the well-intentioned but often amateur earlier Governors.

The 15 post-war years of Dixon's regime were not entirely peaceful. He continued to try to impose his direct rule over the Junior School. In February 1948 Venner was required to present to the Governors regular reports on the Junior School not in person but through Dixon. In July 1953 Dixon said in his own report, 'I have laid down certain rules of discipline for the Junior School and there has been a marked improvement. I have thus broken a tradition of some 30 years.' Early in 1954 the School Inspectors criticised the Junior School, allowing him that July to tell the Governors that he was concerned that 'time was being lost' at the top of the Junior School. Fifteen boys had taken the recent Common Entrance exam when under 13 and he had accepted all but two of them. Next year, before his time was up, Venner resigned.

In these years the Governing Body, despite its new professional members, again missed chances to buy nearby properties which would be invaluable today, including Sir Ernest Roney's house, offered it in 1952 for a mere £5,000, and

Rushmere, next to South Hayes. It did, however, buy a new boarding house. This became necessary when Carrodus, the retired science master, who still owned Glencairn, wanted to turn it into flats. The only suitable alternative the Governing Body could find was 28 Arterberry Road (Weycroft), and on Saturday, 3 June 1948 the chairman and three Governors went to inspect it, but were unable to make an offer because the owner was away. That evening Casswell and Bonn returned and were told that a conveyance to another buyer was ready for signing. Casswell and Bonn then signed a conveyance on behalf of the School and Bonn handed over a personal cheque for the deposit of £1,200.

An embarrassing Governors' meeting followed at which Casswell admitted that he had not had the authority to sign and pointed out that he could lose heavily if he had to buy Weycroft himself then resell it. After much anxious discussion the Governors voted to proceed with the purchase. Weycroft was larger than Glencairn and for 25 years successfully housed sometimes as many as 44 boarders.

Despite its difficulties (of which the outside world knew little and the boys virtually nothing) the School increasingly thrived during the 1950s. Numbers rose steadily, by October 1958 totalling over 800, 500 in the Senior and 300 in the Junior Schools. An increasing number of boys passed School Certificate examinations and won places or scholarships at universities. In June 1952 Dixon reported 'In these days of keen competition it may interest the Governors to know that 9 who wished to go to Oxford and Cambridge have secured entrance through open scholarships or Commoners' entrance examination. Classics 2, Modern Languages 1, History 2, Scientists 2, Biologists 2. These together with our scholars probably make the largest entry in any one year we have ever had to the older universities.' That record was broken in 1955 with 11 Oxbridge scholarships.

Now an unlikely but enormously important consequence of independence was beginning to show itself. The School had lost its direct grant but was continuing to receive support year after year from local government which was sending it so-called 'Surrey scholars', chosen from the cleverest boys in its elementary schools. In 1945 it received 15, next year 20, and from 1947 onwards 25 a year. The part these boys played in raising the School's academic standards can hardly be exaggerated.

The School was also repairing its war-damaged buildings and adding new ones. First came the rebuilding of the gymnasium, then a new science block. The

The completed science blocks in the 1950s. Chronologically (from right): the 1914 block, the 1951 block, and the 1958 block with top storey from a later date.

95

The Film Society in 1955; Jack Smith, founder and organiser seated in the middle.

Governors rejected a flat-roofed building and chose one with a pitched roof to match the 1914 block, which the new block extended to the south and doubled in size. In July 1953 this was ceremonially opened on Commemoration Day – by then an annual event, first announced in 1947 as an 'open day'. Better as the new name sounded, no one has ever been sure what the day commemorates.

The School's out-of-class activities also flourished. Between 1943 and 1949 Peter Beales produced a much admired succession of plays for the Dramatic Society, starting with *Richard of Bordeaux* and including *Sweeney Todd, the Demon Barber*. And in the 1950s two masters, Jack Smith and Robert Holloway, inspired remarkable achievements by the Film Society and the Art Society respectively.

Though the Film Society was only founded in 1948, by 1950 it was claiming to be the most popular in the School, its main activity the showing of such classic films as the Ealing comedies. That summer it also began to make its own films. First was a 12 minute comedy, *Vanishing Tricks*, then *The Owner*, based on a Tolstoy story, though this was never finished because of a post-war shortage of film. In 1952 came *The Wimbledon Hill Mob*.

The unit worked at weekends and would sometimes have as many as 40 actors, two cameramen, and five technicians on the set at a time. In 1953 it made *Time on the Run* and in 1954 *Down to Earth*. Three years later the second of these was awarded an Oscar by the *Amateur Cine World* as one of the ten best amateur productions of the year. Now its premieres were attended by such distinguished members of the film world as Sir John Trevelyan, Dilys Powell, and J. Arthur Rank.

In 1951 the Art Society, originally formed to encourage the appreciation of art, established a printing section, one of its aims to make money by printing

A shot from a Film Society production. The photo is enscribed 'Watson and Mr Watson (no relation)'.

items like School programmes with which to buy reproductions of great paintings. Soon, however, its other aim – fine printing for its own sake – became more important.

Looking back on its early years David Quarrell (1951–6) wrote:

> When I first joined the Press ... we had two machines, one of which was a machine of tremendous proportions. I remember how eagerly we awaited the opportunity of being allowed to operate it. When the next machine came, we were told that it was even larger, and we trod with trepidation lest the floor of the art room should collapse beneath its weight. Now even the magnitude of this machine is eclipsed by our latest acquisition ...
>
> In fact, however, the Art Society Press ... still has the character and aims of the venture which Mr Holloway launched six years ago. No one can miss the friendliness and bustling activity in the art room on Monday afternoons or during the lunch breaks. It would appear to be chaos; there is certainly disorder, but out of that disorder come the books which justify our existence.

Holloway, Hamilton remembered,

> surrounded himself with a gang of about 20 favourites who worked tirelessly for him in out-of-school hours, and I was fortunate enough to be one of them. The Old Art School, a long wooden hut on the north side of the quad with a corrugated roof, was filled with ancient treadle printing presses and heated by two giant Tortoise-style stoves. Tea was on sale at one penny a cup ... He was deeply neurotic, invented imaginary slights and had uncontrollable rages, but if you could cope with that he

*The composing room (*Illustrated London News, *29 October 1960).*

ZEUS was entertaining all the animals at his wedding-feast. Only the tortoise stayed away, and Zeus could not think why. So next day he asked it why it did not come with the others. 'There's no place like home,' it replied—an answer which angered Zeus so much that he made it carry its own house about on its back for the rest of its life.

Many men would rather have plain fare at home than live on the fat of the land in other people's houses.

7

THE GENTLE ART OF PERSUASION

The north wind and the sun were disputing which was the stronger, and agreed to acknowledge as the victor whichever of them could strip a traveller of his clothing. The wind tried first. But its violent gusts only made the man hold his clothes tightly around him, and when it blew harder still the cold made him so

Fine printing by the Art Society Press. Left: Woodcut by Hugh Kolb, from a page of Birds, Beasts, Insects and Plants, 1963-6. Right: Page from Aesop's Fables, printed by the Art Society Press in 1957.

was a lovable chap whose talent and whose ability to find it in others occasionally exposed a genius that he did his best to conceal. … I'm still proud of the work he got out of me: it went far beyond my own estimate of my potential.

Among the Press's most notable productions were *Book of Jugs*, *Aesop's Fables*, and *Jax House*. These two societies came together in 1958 when the film unit made a documentary, *Mondays at Two*, of the Art Society producing a book. There was another connection: Holloway's son, Robin, now a distinguished composer, wrote the music for two of Smith's films.

The Priory as it appeared after a complete rebuilding in 1954–5.

Miles, Head of English from 1951, considered that Dixon's qualities and achievements at King's had been underestimated. Like Rogers, he had 'an outward manner which did not invite intimacy', but, like Rogers, he was basically kind-hearted. Unfortunately he had 'strong and, even for those much more formal times, old-fashioned concepts of authority and demeanour that aroused both derision and resentment'.

As a teacher Dixon's best quality was that he believed in 'stretching pupils' potentialities'. On the other hand he was 'so resolutely determined that a study of Greek and Latin were the religious duty of the ablest boys in the School that he placed unfair pressure on parents and boys to choose the classical Sixth.'

Dixon knew very well what he wanted for the School: 'first-class academic results, a good record at games and an exemplary public image for the boys'. During his later years these were what he was achieving. In all, during his time boys won 145 open awards to Oxbridge. Now, too, its improved sporting standards were being reflected in the successes of its Old Boys. At Oxbridge in these years they won five tennis, four Rugby, three athletic, two rowing, and one cricket blue, as well as seven half-blues. Eight represented England at various sports.

One important reason for the harmony of the 1950s was the good understanding Dixon had with Frank Hole, Chairman of the Governors. Another

Robert Holloway, who founded and ran the Art Society Press.

Cricket, 1950s.

was the fact that by then most of the staff were his own appointments. He had already appointed one of his distinguished successors, Frank Shaw, in the 1930s. Now in 1958 he appointed another, the historian Robin Reeve, and one more future Head, Warwick Hele, who left to teach at Rugby from where he was appointed High Master of St Paul's.

The School's prosperity during these years must stand as one of Dixon's achievements. His true memorial, however, is its independence. Had he not fought so successfully for this it would have had a very different future.

A race in the 1950s.

CHAPTER EIGHT

Shaw's Steady Hand
1960–1975

The year when student protest reached a climax, 1968, came halfway through Frank Shaw's 15-year regime; he arrived for the autumn term of 1960 and left at the end of the summer term, 1975. It was lucky for King's that its Head Master in these years was so civilised and sensible a man.

'Do sit down,' masters would say to each other in the common room. It was the joke of the term, this invitation which Shaw would at once give to masters who came to see him, when previously they might have had to stand for half an hour in front of the Head Master's desk. 'Wait till Shaw comes,' those who had known him in the 1930s had said. Since then he had had wider experience than any previous Head Master. From King's he had gone to teach at Marlborough, both before and after the war. He had then founded a boarding school for the Pakistan Air Force, and more recently been head of Aden College. Dixon's departure was characteristic. He and Shaw talked for half an hour then Dixon said goodbye, leaving Shaw to discover an empty desk. Dixon had destroyed all his own records of the past 26 years.

The flourishing school Shaw nevertheless inherited continued to flourish. In 1961 it won 16 Oxbridge scholarships, in 1965, 25. No longer were boys leaving young; the same year Shaw told his Speech Day audience that half the Senior School were to be found ('occasionally not without diligent searching') in the Sixth.

Its staff still included notable masters from before the war, in particular Peter Gibbs, future head of the Junior School, Duggie Dalziel, Rugby enthusiast, to retire in 1963 after 36 years, by then already for 19 years secretary of the Old King's Club, and Tony Loveband, mathematician, Second Master for 18 years including the whole of Shaw's time, during which he enhanced the importance of this position, said when he retired not only to have made no enemies but never to have been seen to lose his temper.

Frank Howard Shaw, Head Master 1960-75.

Another notable master was John Lecomber (HL to colleagues, 'Cuke' to the boys) who was appointed to King's in 1928 by Rogers. Lecomber took over as Head of Mathematics when Spencer died in 1944, and he remained in that position for over 20 years. He continued teaching the 'double-subject' mathematicians, at first full- and then part-time until 1974. Under his influence, there was a steady stream of boys gaining places and awards to read mathematics at Oxbridge, many demonstrating their love of the subject by continuing their careers as professional mathematicians.

Yet others were the physicist, Mike Smith, about whom Robin Reeve wrote, 'I think the word "brilliant" is not too gross an exaggeration of Mike's teaching. It is true that he was probably less effective with the more ordinary A-level students, but he was, interestingly, always keen to promote the cause of science in the Junior School and for many years ran an annual science tour with Junior School boys'; and Hubert Greenwood, historian, who 'built up the subject from nothing at King's, sending to his old college, Peterhouse, a continuous flow of able historians'. About Greenwood, Roger Lockyer (1941–6) wrote:

> By the time I was preparing for the Peterhouse scholarship examination … flying bombs were falling, and senior boys used to take it in turns to do fire-watching. I spent a number of nights in what was then the Junior School, along with HG. … We took refuge in the cellars of the old house … and would sit opposite each other while we read out and discussed Acton's *Lectures in Modern History*. Looking back on this from fifty years I think it was one of the best possible preparations, and I shall always be grateful to HG for introducing me to these superb essays. But here again … he was a passive partner, listening to what I had to say rather than contributing himself … HG left one free to develop in one's own way and at one's own pace, which is no bad thing.

Neither Smith nor Greenwood confined themselves to their subjects, Smith running the School's successful fencing activities, Greenwood from his arrival in 1934 being Music Master at once establishing a Music Society.

One who, like Smith, arrived after the war was Ian Stewart, to become Head of Modern Languages. About Stewart his successor in that job, Norman Isaacs, has written, 'he brought professionalism to the Department. … He was himself a superb linguist, as authoritative as Fowler in matters of grammar and usage, and possessing a vocabulary of startling breadth, so that he was ever a point of reference and advice for his colleagues. He instilled in his pupils a number of sadly old-fashioned values.' Stewart once confessed himself to Isaacs to be 'an unashamed élitist' and on another occasion 'told me wearily but confidently that "if you stand still long enough, the world will eventually come round again to your position"'. 'To the academically gifted,' Isaacs continued, 'he was a constant source of enlightenment … but he never neglected the weaker boys, for whom – so long as they were ready to work – he had a distinctly soft spot.'

Tennis, golf, squash, swimming, rifle shooting, athletics, and cross-country running as well as fencing had now been added to the School's cricket, Rugby,

Fencing, with cricket in the distance.

A First XV Rugby match.

and hockey playing. 1964 was the hundredth anniversary of Rugby at King's and on 3 December the Junior School celebrated by beating Worth Abbey 49–0. In these hundred years the first Rugby XV had played matches against 52 schools and won over half; boys from 15 foreign countries had played in the XV.

Internal sporting competitions were now between six instead of four houses. By 1958 the old 'district' houses had become too large and boys had been divided (arbitrarily) into six new houses, named after famous masters or Old Boys. 'Major' and 'Maclear' were obvious choices, 'Kingsley' more surprising, since it was the less well-known novelist Henry who had been at the School, the better-known brother Charles at the College.

The Corps, renamed the Combined Cadet Force, with Army, Navy, and RAF sections, was no longer the voluntary/compulsory body it had been before the war, and its members as a result were more committed to warlike or adventurous activities. It had also since 1959 had a rival known as Non Corps Activities. This umbrella name included the old societies, but also new sections undertaking crafts like bookbinding, woodwork, and stage-set construction. By March 1962 it had 162 members, forming 14 sections under 14 masters, and had held its first 'field-day'. A section led by Robin Reeve had spent the day investigating nineteenth-century Battersea. In all there were now some 20 societies, including a Bridge Club a Traditional Jazz Society, and a Ship Study Society. The Film Unit had recently made 'Gunfight at Sapienter', a spoof Western in which the cowboys rode bicycles, and it remained active even after 1962 when Jack Smith was seduced away by Granada Television to run its scientific programmes for schools.

That year the Sixth Form Society was formed, its aim to bring together boys from the different Sixth Forms to hear talks by distinguished visitors. First came Sir John Wolfenden, well known at the time for his report on homosexuality and prostitution. In its third season it was addressed by the Archbishop of Canterbury – the School's Visitor. Though the Archbishop was not universally popular he was a success at King's. 'After a speech lasting just over a minute, Lord

Hockey was only introduced to the School in the 1950s.

Fisher proceeded to keep the attention of the society during a question session of some two hours on such diverse subjects as euthanasia, the established Church and the Church's attitude to war.' Fisher was an experienced schoolmaster, having first taught at Marlborough then been Headmaster of Repton.

King's was also making further improvements to its buildings. Since the 1953 science block the most important of these had been another science block, built in 1957 with the help of an £18,600 grant from the Industrial Fund for the Advancement of Scientific Education; and a new Art School, built in 1959. Here the following year the Art Society Press was preparing its most ambitious project yet: *Graphic Methods*, 100 pages in length.

The School's management was also improving. Astonishingly, it still did not have an official bursar, but G. T. Hamilton-Harding, secretary to the Governing Body for 18 years, was increasingly carrying out a bursar's functions, and when he retired in 1967 his successor, E. W. C. Lambert was given this additional title. The Governing Body had meanwhile formed a Finance and General Purposes Committee, to advise on what should be done with Woodhayes. Its conclusion was to turn the house into staff flats, leaving Shaw (at his own request) to find himself a house. The new committee was better able to plan the use of monies raised by a new appeal, which had been suggested by the fund-raisers, Hooker, Craigmyle, and Co. in 1963, its target the largest yet: £150,000. The buildings planned were a new library, a new dining hall, and a music school, together with eleven modern classrooms, these allowing older ones to be converted into boys' common rooms. All except the music school were opened by Sir John Wolfenden on Commemoration Day, 1967.

The School and house prefects managed their own common rooms, with the result that 'the collage occupying the walls of one room defies description' (Magazine). The Sixth and Fifth Form rooms were managed by committees consisting of a representative from each form, with the Head Master as chairman, in order that 'the bounds of fairly good taste should not be surpassed'.

Though the School was flourishing in so many ways, these were worrying years for its Governors and Head Master, particularly after the election in 1964 of a Labour Government hostile to independent schools. That Speech Day Shaw

Junior School boxing in the gym, repaired after the war damage (Illustrated London News, *1960*).

suggested that the country now had schools of two sorts: Comprehensive and Apprehensive. His speeches on such occasions were never less than entertaining, often brilliant, outshining those of distinguished visitors. Plato, he reminded his audience in 1963, had seen no difficulty in a school leaving age of 35 for the intellectually gifted. Thucydides, he said next year, had recorded that the Athenians defeated in Sicily in the fifth century BC had been offered either slavery in the mines or schoolteaching. In 1966 he reminded them of W. C. Fields' observation that 'no man who hated dogs and children could be altogether bad'. He also recalled (not quite accurately) that it was the centenary of the introduction of confirmation and corporal punishment at King's, 'each in its distinct way efficacious instruments of moral welfare'.

He regularly reassured parents that, in patronising an independent school, they were spending their money wisely and supporting a system which it would be a serious mistake to abolish. State schools might be the chief victims of such an abolition, since independent schools had 'for many years worked against a feeling of complacency in those responsible for the maintained system. ... It would be a strange and unpleasing distinction if in this alone of the countries of the free world it became a criminal offence for parents to spend money on the education of their children.'

Publicly Shaw spoke less of the other worrying development of the 1960s: student protest. Even the Magazine – essentially a conservative organ – now felt that it had a right to comment on the Head Master, observing when Shaw arrived that he inspired 'friendship tempered with respect ... We were particularly pleased to see him at the School Dance, where he remained a remarkably long time, allowing himself to be plied with frequent glasses of hot punch.' About the School's buildings it was equally frank. King's had moved from the Strand 'at a time when the poverty of public taste was in strange contrast with national affluence. The Great Hall and the form rooms below are an unhappy memorial to this... Even the buildings that have been completed since the last war have a disturbingly haphazard air about them: they seem so often to have been sited with an infelicitous lack of overall planning.'

Junior School orchestra, 1960. Concerts at this period were given at least twice a term (Illustrated London News, *1960*).

L-Block buildings 'looking like an air-raid shelter', 1961, later demolished to make way for College Court.

Sixth form chemistry in the 1957 science block (Illustrated London News, *1960*).

In 1968 a long editorial, signed JRE (John Ennals, 1964–9), son of a junior minister in the Labour Government), complained of apathy among the boys of the School. Now, however, two of the School's societies, far from reporting apathy, were experiencing new interest. The Political, Economic, Sociological and Theological Society had been relaunched 'because it was felt that there was a need for a society for discussion, as opposed to mere debate'. On the subject of South Africa's 'ghastly regime ... all points of view, from very extreme right, to even more extreme left, were expressed'. And the Union, now nearly 120 years old, had had to move its meetings to a larger room, where it debated drugs, immigration, and crime and punishment. About its summer 1968 session it reported, 'In a year that is apparently characterised by the violent involvement of the young in political affairs, it is perhaps fortunate for the School that the Union exists as a (more or less) peaceful opportunity for the voicing of partisan sentiments.'

Ennals's editorial suggests one reason for such modest protest at King's. 'We already have ... a great degree of student participation – in the composition of this magazine, the organisation of School societies and games, Charitable Fund, Library and Common Room, as well as in the prefect system.' Shaw's willingness to grant greater democracy and abolish petty rules was even more important. In these years he made prayers voluntary for the second year Sixth Form, so 'tending to reduce the element of opposition from the back of the Hall'. And he encouraged the Common Room Committees when they became the Sixth Form Committee. By the end of the year this had produced for itself a constitution, which laid down as one of its functions 'to hold meetings with the Headmaster in order to discuss proposals put forward by the Committee'. Reporting on these meetings, the secretary, Richard Stoate (1966–70), wrote that the Head Master 'wholeheartedly supported our progress. ... The strength of any body such as this lies not in "sit-ins" and "lock-outs" but in a productive liaison between Headmaster and Students and we are extremely fortunate in this respect.'

If the Committee's achievements (suits instead of uniform for the Lower Sixth, permission for its members to leave the School during the lunch break) hardly seem earth shaking, they indicate Shaw's conciliatory attitude. The School's prefects, indeed, considered the new committee dangerously radical. In 1969 William Petch (1963–9, Captain of the School and joint editor of the Magazine) wrote that it seemed 'to have evolved into a body wishing to alter the very foundations of the School, by a series of radical reforms.... They originally came into being in order to look after the Common Rooms. ... This they sadly failed to do, and the Common Rooms, apart from the radios installed from the outset, remain as mere lockerrooms. Where . ... is the table tennis so rashly promised to us by this eminent body some time ago?'

Geography lesson (Illustrated London News, *1960*).

By the summer of 1969 Shaw considered that permissiveness had gone far enough and said so on Speech Day. The School had been 'right to review the need for certain restrictive rules that make little sense today. But ... their concern must now be that the rules that remained should be obeyed.' It had been a year when

the National Union of Students had turned a paternal eye on the VI forms with an exciting invitation to join in a movement for the abolition of virtually everything and the substitution of government by Student Councils.

No one could wish to condemn the young, however exasperating, to the experience of permanent, frustrating and futile committee procedure.

As for the two recent reports, Newsom and Donnison, and the plethora of advice on education,

Those who taught hardly knew whether to feel gratitude or despair that, alone of professions, they were the recipients of vast quantities of advice. The sincerity and good intentions of most of the freelance experts was not doubted, but one envied them the revelation of certainty and truth that lack of practical experience afforded them, and regretted that their glimpses of the obvious were so darkened by obscurity of language. 'The right of being obscure,' Ruskin had said, 'is not one to be lightly claimed. It can only be founded on long efforts to be intelligible.' At least the School now knew that the Government did not mean to legislate against fee-paying schools, and should be grateful for that, even if it came dangerously close to the injunction. 'Thou shalt not kill but needst not strive officiously to keep alive.'

In practice Shaw continued to make changes which could be called progressive, one of them the abolition of Speech Days, a surprising decision considering the good impression he always created at these. Another (in 1969) transformed the Drama Society by inviting the pupils of Wimbledon High School for Girls to take part. The first joint effort, that perennial favourite of dramatic societies, *The Crucible* (hardly stageable without girls), was considered by the Magazine to be the best production for years. Girls from the same school were soon playing in King's orchestras.

Shaw also extended student–staff consultation by creating a School Council, to consist of members elected from each age-group, with a master to act as its

School play, 1960s. All plays were in the Great Hall until Collyer Hall was built.

107

speaker. In essence this was a more widely based Sixth Form Committee. It was soon, in Shaw's opinion, making 'many positive recommendations'. And in 1970 he appointed the Senior School's first woman teacher, an American mathematician, A. S. Friedman.

Next year Shaw himself went with a Russian-speaking master and a group of boys to Leningrad and Moscow. Other European visits were now regular, but this was the first to Russia. In 1974 a much larger group went to the USA.

Most important of all innovations, however, was the introduction in 1970 of a Tutor System. Every boy would now have a staff tutor to watch over his progress throughout his time at the School and to meet and know his parents. Tutors were to have responsibility for about 15 boys. Without doubt the Tutor System was to have a greater effect on the nature of the School than any other organisational change.

Meanwhile, the Governing Body had been planning ahead. It was jolted into taking a longer view of the future when it faced three simultaneous problems: what to do with Woodhayes, now divided into staff flats which had to be subsidised; what to do with Weycroft, now becoming uneconomic as a boarding house; and what to do with the Lodge. In 1961 F. A. Strickland, the owner of this largish house standing west of the original South Hayes but also backing on the playing fields, had given the school the right to buy it on his death for £10,000. Now that he had died the price was so much below its current value that relatives went to court to have the arrangement nullified, but they were unsuccessful and in 1971 the Lodge was bought by the School.

Governors Jules Collyer (1924–7) and Graeme Cranch were asked to solve these problems, and as a result of their report the Governing Body established a Planning Committee, with Collyer as its chairman. After 18 months this Committee which included the two Head Masters, Cranch and two other masters, produced a 150-page report with 150 pages of appendices, covering everything which it foresaw the School becoming and needing during the next ten years.

Among adopted proposals were the sale of Woodhayes and Weycroft in order to raise money for more essential buildings. These should include yet more, badly needed science laboratories. It was Collyer, with his knowledge of the building industry, who saw that they could be created not by building at ground level but within the pitched roofs of the existing science blocks – a feature which the Governing Body had insisted on for aesthetic reasons. The Lodge itself could not be altered externally for 20 years, but was converted first for use by the music department, then for a boarding house, while its gardens were made into six hard tennis-courts.

Administratively the most significant changes recommended by the report were the creation of a permanent Building Committee, and of a Head Master's Liaison Group. This last was to be made up of the two Head Masters, four Governors, and eight rotating members of the two Schools' staffs.

In 1973 Frank Hole died of a heart attack while watching the Ryder Cup meeting at Gleneagles. He had been Chairman for 23 years and was the most liked and quietly successful the School had had. He had been largely responsible for the peace between Dixon and his staff during the 1950s, and since then had

The Head Master starting a cross-country race.

had an excellent relationship with Shaw (doing all this for the School while at the same time managing British Rail's hotel division and sitting on the boards of numerous companies). He was succeeded by Cavan Taylor (1948–53), a 37-year-old City solicitor, later senior partner at Lovell, White, and Darrent.

Shaw, meanwhile, had been elected Chairman of the Headmasters' Conference for 1972, a rare honour for a day school headmaster which reflected the respect felt for him throughout the teaching world. His wide popularity among boys, staff, and Governors ignored one failing. In a way he was too tolerant, allowing certain masters to remain when they should have been eased into retirement. Some taught nothing because they had no control. In the classroom of one, boys used to cook on a primus stove. Double doors had to be fitted to a science block classroom to prevent the chaos within making teaching impossible in nearby classrooms. Boys of the time name five masters who were too old, shell-shocked, or alcoholic to be teachers. Shaw can hardly have been unaware of these problems. 'We are a profession,' he would say, 'in which you look after someone with a broken wing.'

As a whole, however, he left the School in excellent shape; in his 15 years no fewer than 199 open awards were won at Oxbridge. His still greater achievement was to steer King's peacefully through the 1960s. He was as admired a Head Master as Rogers had been and more universally liked.

CHAPTER NINE

A Difficult Time
1975–1980

Christopher Wightwick, Head Master 1975–80.

The appointment of Christopher Wightwick as Shaw's successor was a strange affair. A selection committee of the Governing Body shortlisted three from 51 applicants and the Governors were to interview them on 16 November 1974, but by then two had withdrawn, Wightwick alone remaining. The chairman of the selection committee offered to repeat the selection process, if the Governors wished, but they were well satisfied with Wightwick.

He was the first Head Master of King's not to be a classicist. After teaching languages at two lesser public schools he had become Sixth Form German master then Head of Modern Languages at Westminster, and he came with a strong recommendation from Westminster's Head, John Rae. His interests were wide – photography, painting, architecture; in these he claimed to have achieved 'a fine standard of mediocrity'.

While the School continued in most respects to run effectively there is no denying that Wightwick's four and a half years as Head Master were controversial. In June 1976 the Governing Body recorded in its minutes, 'The headmaster reported that he would make it a matter of future policy to insist on masters retiring at sixty.' Innocuous as this sounds, it is the iceberg tip of a relationship between Wightwick and certain of his senior staff which in the end proved fatal.

To Wightwick it seemed when he arrived that King's was an old-fashioned school, in need of modernising. Most obviously, certain masters whom Shaw had protected should be replaced. Right as this policy may have been, he carried it out with insufficient tact.

Changes which Wightwick made to the shape of the School contributed to the unhappiness some felt. As part of a general reshaping of the Middle School he increased the numbers of sets which took three years rather than two to prepare for GCE O-level exams. In the mid-1980s King's along with other London independent schools adopted this pattern for pupils, but at the time some staff saw the change as a downgrading of King's academic traditions. Many, however, strongly supported it and had advocated it long before.

He was similarly ahead of his time in broadening the Middle School curriculum to include more subjects and reduce early specialisation, a change made by all schools when they adopted the national curriculum, but gave offence, for example, by telling the Head of Chemistry, without previous consultation, that boys were no longer to be required to take all three science subjects. He was, in the words of his successor, inclined to charge into change rather than ease into it when the need became indisputable. It was particularly unwise to give the impression that he meant to change so much when Shaw had been such an admired Head Master.

More generally, Wightwick adopted an informality of behaviour (attending the confirmation service in casual clothes, sitting on the table at Assembly) which older masters considered inappropriate. Today accompanying boys on cross country runs would at worst seem an imitation of American Presidential behaviour, but in the 1970s at King's it seemed to conservative masters to be incompatible with a headmaster's dignity. If Wightwick's miscalculation was to underestimate the cumulative power of staff opposition, his misfortune was that he was not Shaw. Boys, on the other hand, approved. They liked Wightwick's formal abolition of corporal punishment (in practice rarely used in Shaw's time), his introduction of more women teachers, and his reform of assemblies – substituting debates or talks by visiting speakers for 'the lacklustre attempts ... to sing morning hymns – not many of us being sufficiently awake at this time'. They liked the increased contacts he encouraged with Wimbledon High School for Girls, his positive attempts to know boys by having them photographed individually, his approachability and willingness to respond to particular boys' needs, and in general what they saw as his success in taking the School 'out of the 1950s ethos' without compromising its academic integrity.

If the boys also approved of the younger teachers he introduced, it is some of the older ones whom they name as the best of their time, in particular Frank Miles, Head of English. In the 1950s Clive Hamilton remembered that, 'Even clause analysis was an exciting business in Frank Miles's English classes. His whole attention was constantly focused on the entire class who, left with no opportunity to talk to each other, ended up learning a lot.' Twenty years later Francis Topping (1969–73) remembered that 'Pupils queued early to get into his classroom ... He mesmerised us with his humour and ability with language.' By the time Miles retired in 1983 after 33 years at King's 130 of his boys had gained Oxbridge awards or places, and 15 were teaching at various universities. His subsequent work on the School's history has made the present history possible.

Another outstanding master of the time, appointed by Shaw, was Norman Isaacs, later to become Head of Modern Languages. The present Head Master, Robin Reeve, has described him as 'one of the most distinguished Heads of Modern Languages whom I have met in my career ... a huge enthusiast for French and German literature and someone who has also embraced the modern approach without losing any of his belief in grammatical rigour.'

Cavan Taylor, Chairman of the Governing Body, 1973–90.

Others again were Colin Evans, Senior Master, a Welshman from Middlesex, geographer and later Head of Geography and Economics, described by Reeve as 'an enormous enthusiast for his subject and tremendous performer in the classroom'. And Bryan Stokes, Head of Chemistry, then the School's first Head of Science. He was to play a leading part not only in the development of the School's science, but nationally in his work on the Nuffield chemistry project. It was typical of common room loyalty to the School that when Stokes retired in 1993 after 41 years he became Secretary of the Old King's Club.

Short as Wightwick's stay was, it saw important developments at King's. Between 1976 and 1980 further items from the 1972 Development Plan were transformed into bricks and tile, most importantly the new premises for the Junior School. These were created in three stages: first the building of the music school, second the building of a new classroom block, third the refurbishing and extending of the Priory. On 26 January 1980 the Junior School finally occupied its new buildings. All its boys, by this time 380 of them, could now be taught in their own classrooms in a single group of buildings surrounding their own quadrangle, the renovated Priory its central feature.

For this and other purposes an appeal had been launched to be overseen by Frank Smith, the Governor who more than any other was responsible for professionalising the School's financial affairs. At his memorial service in 1987 Cavan Taylor remembered that when he had first become a Governor and Frank Hole was chairman, Smith had already been something of an '*éminence grise*'. Hole would take no important decision without consulting Smith, who for 15 years dominated the Finance and General Purposes Committee. As a member of a subcommittee set up to amend the School's statutes, Taylor remembered: 'I suppose we all had about half a dozen suggested amendments except Frank Smith who probably had around 200. Barely a section had survived unscathed his industrious and fluent pen. It was suggested that I should be sent to the Department of Education and Science to negotiate the amendments and when I protested to Frank that there was not a hope of getting all that he had proposed he said, "That's quite right but if you press them you'll probably get the half dozen we all want".' The buildings and bursaries appeal which Smith promoted in the late 1970s raised over half a million pounds.

Another innovation which brought the School money, if in more modest amounts, was the establishment of the Friends of KCS. Such a group had been proposed in 1916 by Governor Alfred Pollard (father of the first Old Boy to die in the 1914–18 War). In 1976 the Friends were at last founded, their aim to draw together all who wished the School well and were willing to give it financial and moral support. During its first five years it raised a total of £30,000, much of it 'painlessly from "fun" occasions': dances, parties, and lectures. Its only failure had been to raise enough for the building of squash courts – a failure probably for the best, since the site now chosen, next to the Sports Hall, is a better one than the abandoned site near the swimming-pool.

In 1979 the School celebrated its 150th anniversary, sharing the occasion with London Transport and the Metropolitan Police. Numerous special events were staged. In January the Nobel Prize winner, Professor M. H. F. Wilkins, lectured

to the Sixth Form Society. In February the School Visitor, Archbishop D. D. Coggan, visited the School. In March the School's Choral Society sang Bach's *B Minor Mass* at Southwark Cathedral. The following term in May, the Friends of KCS held a ball, and on Commemoration Day, as usual, cricket, tennis, shooting, and swimming matches took place against the Old Boys. In the autumn term, a large gathering of Old Boys attended an anniversary dinner; the Bishop of Southwark, Mervyn Stockwood, conducted a service of thanksgiving and dedication at St Mary's, Wimbledon; and the School competed with Old Boys at that King's speciality, cross-country running. There were many other dramatic, musical, and sporting events and, the same year, Frank Miles and Graeme Cranch published *King's College School: The First 150 Years*.

Wightwick's problems had begun early. He had been Head Master for less than a year when in June 1976 Michael Smith, Head of Physics, wrote to him:

London Transport shared in the School's 150th anniversary celebrations, 1979. Sir Jeremiah Colman had given Woodhayes to the School in 1931.

Judo was introduced to the School in 1971.

Although you no doubt have the right, as Head Master, to introduce widespread changes irrespective of staff opinion, I do not believe that you can run the school as effectively without staff support. It appears to me that you take a number of decisions on your own in circumstances in which prior consultation with the staff would be desirable. However carefully you may try to predict the consequences of your actions, there are likely to be a number of occasions on which second or further opinions may reveal possibilities that you have not considered.

Before the end of the year the Governors called Peter Kirman, Second Master, and Colin Evans, Senior Master, to meet them privately. Already they were considering whether Wightwick should go, but Kirman and Evans argued that this was premature and unfair, and nothing was done.

On their own many of the matters about which the staff complained seem trivial. When Colin Evans listed 21 changes, ranging from the popular to the controversial, made by Wightwick in his first year the change against which Evans noted 'extremely unpopular, much strong feeling' was 'Relaxation of uniform rules'. A year later (December 1977) Wightwick overruled an attempt by housemasters to forbid the wearing of flamboyant scarves and insist on School ones.

Eventually a small group of senior members of staff wrote letters of complaint to the Governing Body. In the opinion of Colin Holloway – one of Wightwick's most perspicacious appointments as head of the Junior School – these letters were not so much the precipitation of the crisis as the confirmation the Governing Body required to support a view the majority of them had already formed of Wightwick's headmastership. They were marked confidential, and in Wightwick's opinion the Governing Body should have returned them, saying that nothing could be done unless it was allowed to discuss them with the Head Master. Instead he was asked to resign.

The masters who had written to the Governors by no means represented a unanimous common room. On 12 September 1978 a group of 'senior office holders' wrote to the chairman of the Governors:

> 1. We think that the Governors should know that we believe that the evidence on which the Governors have acted, as it has been related to us by Christopher Wightwick, has been incomplete and unbalanced; 2. the judgement passed on Christopher Wightwick's tenure of the post, as we have been told it, has been in some elements underinformed and is therefore unfair; 3. the action taken has been so precipitate as to be likely in itself to cause grave danger to the School.

Nevertheless Wightwick agreed to resign and it was only during 1979 that he realised how much support he had, not only from boys and masters, but from a group of parents who formed an Action Committee to defend him. As a result he decided to withdraw his resignation, but when the Governing Body met on 12 October it voted 19 to 5 with one abstention not to agree to his doing so. The brief passage in the Governors' minute-book recording this vote is the first mention it makes of a crisis which by then had continued for some three years.

Wightwick's resignation did not end the matter. The local press reported what it described as a standing ovation the boys gave him at his final assembly, and identified Governor Mervyn Stockwood as his main defender and Sir Cyril Black MP as leader of his opponents. Meanwhile 16 masters had written to Stockwood, 'The following members of the staff of King's College School, Wimbledon, would like to state their opinion that, whatever reservation individuals may have about CCB Wightwick's qualities as Head Master, the suggestion that he has proved unable to work harmoniously with his staff as a whole is untrue.' There were also protests from some parents during the next Corporation meeting at the Governing Body's treatment of Wightwick.

Holloway considers that 'of the issues Wightwick propounded, most have come to fulfilment' and that he 'deserves credit for perceiving the needs', but admits ruefully that he was 'the wrong man in the wrong place at the wrong time'. Certainly Wightwick regrets that he was not allowed more time, believing that he was beginning to overcome his difficulties. 'He was too liberal for his time, and made a number of errors of judgement,' says Cavan Taylor, chairman of the Governors throughout these years.

An interregnum followed Wightwick's departure, during which Peter Kirman, the Second Master, became Acting Head Master, a man respected by the whole common room, who throughout the previous four years had done much to calm emotions and who now helped to heal the rift between common room factions. In the words of Robin Reeve, Kirman, 'as well as being an outstanding teacher of mathematics, was a man of complete integrity, totally without side, with a scorn of gossip'. In the years to come it was he, Reeve, who decided 'the broad direction in which the School should go', but it was Kirman who would devise ways in which to make this happen. When Kirman retired in 1992 the applause at his final assembly showed that the boys, too, recognised his qualities.

CHAPTER TEN

Consolidation and Growth
1980–1995

Though the Headmasters' Conference advised its members not to apply to succeed Wightwick, there were 77 applicants in 1979 for the headmastership of King's. The four shortlisted candidates were submitted to an intense scrutiny by the selection committee of the Governing Body, which was determined to establish their attitudes to such vital issues as the relationship between the Head Master and senior members of his staff. The choice of Robin Reeve has been triumphantly vindicated. He was a distinguished scholar with a First Class in both parts of the History Tripos at Cambridge and well known to Governors from his time at the School during the 1950s and 1960s, when he had been a main force in the history department and had encouraged a broad approach to the subject through, for example, the History Society. Since then he had been Head of History and Director of Studies at Lancing. In a sense he may have been the Governors' safe choice. He has turned out to be a great deal more than this.

Despite the manifest problems of the previous administration the day-to-day running of the School continued relatively undisturbed. Nevertheless it had been an unpleasant episode and morale might have deteriorated. Perhaps with this in mind the staff set aside existing differences and united in welcoming the new Head Master. Reeve showed tact and firmness in handling the situation. It was not long before he had gained the loyalty and respect of staff and boys.

Crucial though this may have been, it was only a necessary preliminary to Reeve's plans for the School. Foremost among these was that it should consolidate and enhance its academic reputation. There was a problem here, in that the last of the Surrey Scholars, who had been responsible for so many of

Robin Reeve, Head Master, on his appointment in 1980.

Opposite page: *The new quadrangle.*

its academic successes over the past 35 years, were now leaving the School. In future two-thirds of the Senior School boys would continue to come from the Junior School and could be expected to be excellent, but more of the rest would come from local preparatory schools, and, judging by the past, would be of mediocre quality. Shaw, supported by the intake of Surrey Scholars, had had less need to address this problem. Reeve now undertook a carefully planned campaign to attract the attention of the headmasters of local preparatory schools. The links between them and King's became closer and more friendly, with the result that many of their best pupils began to come to the School. So effective was this that by 1994 no Common Entrance candidate either from the Junior School or elsewhere scored under 70 per cent and a substantial number of King's Entrance Scholars also came from neighbouring schools.

In parallel with this Reeve set about a fundamental upgrading of the School's buildings. He was the first Head Master with a vision of the kind of buildings the School deserved to match its historical and academic standing. Previously there had been a tendency to view each extension in isolation, with little idea of how it would contribute to the whole, or thought for what might follow.

Interestingly one of his first decisions was to open a small school chapel. A room in South Hayes was chosen for the purpose and the project was enthusiastically supported by both the Friends of KCS and Old Boys. The Chapel of Christ the King was dedicated by the Bishop of Southwark on 12 May 1983.

The refurbishment of the Great Hall was already under discussion when Reeve arrived. Serious work began in 1988 after the opening of Collyer Hall when it became possible to remove the stage. The panelling was then renovated, the gallery was constructed, the floor renewed and the brick and stone work cleaned. In 1994 the climax to the project was reached with the installation of the restored Conacher organ from Lockwood Parish Church, Huddersfield on the gallery. The magnificent casework of the organ, and its distinctive quality as an instrument make it a worthy enhancement of the Great Hall.

An urgent strategic concern was the Development Plan. This was given to Reeve with the clear implication that it was irrevocable. But he decided to rethink it from first principles. To follow the Junior School complex the plan's next major item was to be a sports hall on the site of the existing Junior School assembly hall and the ugly L-shaped block of form rooms hastily thrown up in Shaw's time. Reeve realised that a hangar-like building situated in the very centre of the School would ruin its appearance from the south besides robbing it of the last significant area available for further academic buildings. He therefore persuaded the Governing Body to use instead the garden of the Lodge, at that time the School's boarding house.

The Sports Hall was ready for the summer term of 1984. It cost £885,000 and provided indoor areas for tennis, badminton, volleyball, basketball, fencing and cricket practice as well as all kinds of physical education. Inevitably

Rugby, 1987. Collyer Hall is being constructed in the background.

local sporting clubs wanted to use it. Far from proving a difficulty, this has been of benefit to the School, and led to the establishment of KCS Enterprises, a company which manages the letting of all School buildings and grounds. In 1993 it had a turnover of £60,000, expected to rise to £100,000. Its profits go to the School.

The development of the gymnasium and adjacent area followed. Originally the central purpose was to provide a new assembly hall for the Junior School, but the new buildings eventually included a Sixth Form Centre and the hall was redesigned so that it could also be a theatre. College Court, as the Sixth Form building was named (to commemorate the historic link with the College), was not intended to isolate Sixth Formers from the rest of the School: much of their teaching still takes place in the classrooms and laboratories which other forms use. On the other hand it does give them their own study and recreation areas, and represents a promotion to which younger boys can look forward throughout their school lives. In addition to extra classrooms, a careers department, a large common room and a spacious reading room, College Court also accommodates the computer and economics departments. The building has been run since its opening by Alan Thomas.

The theatre/hall, completed a year earlier at a cost of about £900,000 and named Collyer Hall after Governor Jules Collyer, the main force behind the original Development Plan and for 17 years chairman of the Building Committee, consists primarily of a theatre equipped to professional standards but is also flexible enough to provide for a wide range of drama from the youngest to the Sixth Form.

For years all plays had been produced in the Great Hall, with its high, restricted stage reached only by an almost perpendicular ladder from the classroom below. There were no real changing or make-up rooms.

Opposite page: The Collyer Hall theatre (above), and (below) the swimming pool.

The second rebuilding of the Priory, 1980–1.

Nevertheless many much admired plays had been produced there, especially under Norman Isaacs, Head of Modern Languages, and John Evans, subsequently Senior Master. When Robin Reeve returned to King's in 1980 Isaacs and Evans had already been producing 'the major School play for many years and the quality of these performances certainly was astonishingly good'. The new theatre was a fitting recognition of the standards achieved in drama at the School. It has proper make-up and storage areas and a modern control room. Hall and theatre were formally opened by Lord St John of Fawsley on 18 November 1988, the opening followed by the staging of Feydeau's *A Little Hotel on the Side*, the main event in a festival fortnight which, under the Director of Collyer Hall, Philip Swan, has become a biennial opportunity to bring leading names into the School, as well as providing a special challenge to its own performers!

At about the same time as the building of Collyer Hall, the swimming pool, originally built in the mid-1930s, was enclosed, the roof at first intended to last ten years, but upgraded during planning so that it is now expected to last 20 or even 30. Today it has become an essential centre for PE and leisure use.

The impression created by the face-lift King's was given in the 1980s is suggested by Roy Plomley (inventor of 'Desert Island Discs') in his account of the Gaudy he attended for boys of the 1930s.

> What fun it was going to be to see again the little tuckshop where we queued outside the window through which the Steward dispensed chocolate and ice cream, and the House Rooms, scene of so many remembered rags, and the old corrugated iron art studio, and the tennicoit courts, and the flowered patch belonging to the Gardening Society, from which I had been asked to leave after squirting the hose at a fellow member. But they had all gone! The school I was being shown was magnificent but almost unrecognisable. A computer room! – a vast indoor sports centre! – music studios! … we had known nothing like this.

When he wrote, Collyer Hall and the Sixth Form Centre were still to come.

So were other expansions, forced on the Governing Body by opportunities which might never recur, most importantly the acquisition of Rushmere, the large house standing immediately east of the original South Hayes house. Reeve was determined that this was a house which the School ought to buy if the opportunity arose. He came to know David Wynne, the well-known sculptor and owner of Rushmere, and told him the School was seriously interested in the house. In 1991 the School was offered and bought Rushmere.

Complicated discussions followed about what to do with it. The two Head Masters and the Governors considered the possibility of using it for a pre-prep school with an entry age of four, but recognised that not only would it be impossible to make a proper judgement about a boy's potential at that age, but the parents would expect such a school to take girls. This would not be right

Opposite page: *One of Robin Reeve's first decisions as Head Master was to open a school chapel* (above). Below: *the Senior School library.*

The rebuilt Priory.

as long as the Junior and Senior Schools did not take them, a possibility considered by the Governing Body in 1992 but rejected. In the end it was decided on the Junior School Head Master's advice to lower the School's entry age to seven and use Rushmere for two classes of seven-year-olds and four classes of eight-year-olds. Though Rushmere and its classes remain part of the Junior School, it has been given a separate identity, and is supervised by a member of staff known as Master in Rushmere – 'very baronial', wrote Colin Holloway.

The arrangement not only enlarged the School, so enabling it to cover the mortgage on Rushmere, but offered places to suitable boys at an age when they might otherwise had been taken by preparatory schools. It also provided a less formidable introduction to the School for eight- as well as seven-year-olds than the Priory, for, by 1993, the Junior School numbered 460, making it one of the largest preparatory schools in the country.

In the early 1990s the School also took the opportunity to buy Barclays Bank's fine boathouse on the Thames at Putney; several other institutions were interested but the King's bid was successful. And in these years the chance also came to provide Old Boys with a permanent pavilion at West Barnes Lane, when their temporary pavilion was burned down. The new pavilion is shared with the Old Boys of Christ's Hospital, who sold adjoining land there to King's to raise their part of the building costs.

Earl Jellicoe opening the rebuilt Junior School.

In the 1980s King's faced a problem which all day schools have faced sooner or later: whether to retain Saturday morning school. This had been discussed in Wightwick's time, but the Governing Body had resisted change. In 1982 when it was raised again the more conservative Governors held the same view, but agreed to set up a working party. By this time the School's boarding house was due to be closed, so removing one objection to a five day week, and when the working party reported the following June this was what it recommended. It was Reeve's anxiety that Saturday classes would have to be held on Monday afternoons, traditionally reserved for out-of-school activities, a feature of King's which he thought special and important. By adding a sixth period on Monday and Friday mornings this was avoided and Monday (later Friday) afternoons preserved for the School's extra-curricular activities.

Neither the five day week, nor another important change, the replacement of rigid streaming with 'setting' by ability in particular subjects, have had the adverse effects on the School's academic standards which some feared. These also survived the various educational changes which came in quick succession during the 1980s: the introduction of GCSE exams and the national curriculum, and the modification of special entry arrangements for Oxford and Cambridge. Indeed, the 1990s league tables, however interpreted, have consistently put King's in the top 15 schools, placing it clearly among the country's leading academic schools.

Meanwhile extra-curricular activities thrived and music became a special feature. By 1994 400 boys were receiving instrumental or voice tuition from 24 of the best peripatetic London music teachers. As well as Junior, Second, and First Orchestras it had two wind bands, a chamber choir, and a School choir. Choral music has indeed become a special feature, first under John Carol Case who became a professional singer, next under Noel Long, later responsible for the Ernest Read Children's Concerts, then under Michael Jenkins. The increasingly renowned Chamber Choir has successfully toured France, Italy and Wales – as well as performing in the main London concert halls. Similarly the Art Department has flourished in recent years. Its activities include a multiplicity of exhibitions in both painting and ceramics and have achieved correspondingly excellent output both in terms of the quality of work and examination results. Unlike art, design and technology only began to flourish at KCS in the 1980s, when the building to accommodate it was opened next to the art school.

During the 1980s the Magazine finally achieved style. In 1975 it had become an annual, and by 1983 the editor was complaining that there was 'a bewildering reluctance among our readers to provide the sort of material that would rebut the charge that the Magazine does little more than print games reports'. Two years later, however, it not only had a features section of articles and poetry, but also an enlivened sports section with profiles and photographs. John Cole, the BBC political editor and father of three boys at the School, had contributed an article on 'The Politics of Education'. By 1989 a still fatter magazine had a spine and glossy cover.

Robin Reeve and Colin Holloway outside the newly acquired boathouse in Putney.

Colin Holloway, Headmaster of the Junior School.

The School remains unusual in devoting an afternoon to extra-curricular activities. In addition to the long-established CCF there is now a strong tradition of community service with an emphasis on work among young people with physical or psychological disabilities or other special educational needs. The Chaplain, Robin Stevens, now runs a charity, based on the School and the parish, to provide food and clothing for some of London's homeless.

From the mid-1960s cricket has perhaps been the School's most consistently successful sport, played on one of the finest school grounds in the London area. An outstanding player from the earlier years of this period, when David Belchamber, later the Bursar, was in charge, was Dudley Owen-Thomas. After captaining the XI in 1967 he became a leading batsman for Cambridge and played regularly for Surrey. Another happy period was the 1970s and 1980s under Andrew Lang, later Second Master, with Reg Dare, the former Hampshire player as professional. Although there had been previous cricket tours of Holland, new ground was broken in 1989 when the School team took part in the Sir Garfield Sobers tournament in Barbados. First-class cricketers from the school in the 1980s and 1990s were Andrew Bredin (Sussex), Rehan Alikhan (Sussex and Surrey), and Marcus Wight (Gloucestershire). In 1993 Russell Cake, like Wight a Cambridge blue, scored a century for the Combined Universities against the Australians.

Wight and Cake also won hockey blues for Cambridge, as did Guy and Richard Slimmon, one at Cambridge, one at Oxford. The sport has developed strongly at the School since the laying of the artificial grass pitch at West Barnes Lane in 1989. Richard Luddington, now a Governor, was another to win a hockey blue. Luddington was a gifted all-rounder, also winning

124

cricket and Rugby blues at Oxford. The outstanding Rugby side of the 1980s was probably that of 1988, which won 14 of its 18 matches. A powerful influence on KCS rugby since he joined the Common Room in 1976 has been Bob Hiller, seven times Captain of England between 1969 and 1972. Other Rugby highlights of the 1980s were a Rugby tour of California where the XV won all its matches and a Rugby-rowing tour of New Zealand and Fiji, where the XV lost all but one, though the oarsmen did better. Rowing was a sport at which King's excelled throughout these years, and so too was tennis in which the School has enjoyed consistent competitive success under the direction of Ralph Cake, now Senior Housemaster. 1991 was a particularly fine

Music out of doors, 1980s.

125

Biology field course, 1989.

year when KCS crews won four gold medals at the National Schools' Championships.

KCS has always excelled at tennis, often competing successfully in the Glanville and Youll cups. Buster Mottram, who left in 1978, played in the Wimbledon championships while still at school, and was later one of the most successful of British players at Wimbledon since the war and a regular member of the Davis Cup team.

In 1987 the Junior School celebrated its seventy-fifth anniversary. Since the war it had grown steadily. Landmarks include the acquisition of the Priory in 1946, its rebuilding in 1954, the great expansion in numbers caused by difficulties experienced by local preparatory schools, and its complete rehousing during the second half of the 1970s.

In 1965 J. R. Diver, who had succeeded Venner as Head of the Junior School, was himself succeeded by Peter Gibbs. Gibbs had been recruited 30 years earlier by Wood-Hill and in all stayed 41 years at the School, only absent three times: for war service, when his house was bombed, and for mumps. Inevitably some of his prejudices were those of earlier times, but this did not prevent him supporting Shaw in handling tactfully the unrest of the late 1960s.

Other Junior School masters who had given long and devoted service during the Junior School's first 75 years included John Rosser, who deputised as Head when Diver was ill for a term. About Rosser, David Jones, the present Second Master, has written: 'his influence was outstanding in this role and there were few among the boys or staff who did not experience his encouragement and sympathy'. In 1978 Rosser was succeeded by a partnership between Algy Sinclair and Bill Llewellyn, 'one organising the staff with dry

Archery, 1990.

humour, the other firmly but kindly taking charge of the boys'. They were followed by another successful partnership between Jones and Tony Hein, whose services to the Junior School and the Old Boys were recognised by his election in 1986 as a Vice-President of the Old King's Club.

Before Gibbs left he drew up plans for the Junior School's needs during the imminent rebuilding. His successor, Colin Holloway, who came from King's earliest rival, University College School, and arrived just before the reconstruction began, wrote about the old L-Block of classrooms, 'It seemed to burrow into the ground as it approached South Hayes as though uncertain whether it was an air-raid shelter left from the last war or aspired to be a fall-out bunker for the next.' About the rebuilt Junior School, finally opened by Earl Jellicoe in 1980, Holloway wrote that it provided excellent accommodation 'without the massive blocks and echoing institutional corridors that spoil so many new school buildings. The scale is right for the younger boys....'

All Junior School boys are prepared to take Common Entrance during the academic year in which they become 13, and this means that the 11-year-old entrants from state schools must be given special science, Latin and French teaching. Each year nearly 100 go to the Senior School, compared to a little over 50 who come from elsewhere; these numbers suggest how vital a part it plays in maintaining the high academic standards of the School as a whole, as well as enjoying a full and distinctive programme of its own.

The Senior School also benefits from receiving so many boys who have already adapted to the KCS style they are to be taught, and have some understanding of the culture of the School. On the other hand, the boys of the Junior School enjoy the important benefits of being able to use Senior School science, cultural and sporting facilities of a sort which few preparatory schools

Robin Reeve, 1994.

can provide. Musically, they form part of the School's choruses at a time when choral singing has become one of the Music Department's specialities. In such ways the two schools are a single school, but at the same time they remain what they have been since Rogers installed Wood-Hill in 1912: separate and self-managing.

As the Junior and Senior Schools have grown in size both headmasters in the '90s have extended their management teams. In the Senior School the position of Senior Housemaster was introduced in 1983 when John Davies was appointed to it. The appointment of the first Director of Studies, Ken Durham, followed in 1992. In Andrew Lang as Second Master and John Evans as Senior Master, King's is served in the '90s by two long-serving teachers very much in the tradition established by Tony Loveband and Peter Kirman.

Few headmasters of independent schools in this century have failed to see problems ahead, and Reeve is no exception. If political suppression was yesterday's threat, today's he believes could be the self-governing state school, as keen as any independent school to compete academically. Independent day schools cannot take too much comfort from the way in which they have survived the recession of the early 1990s better than boarding schools. They too must demonstrate that what they have to offer is worth its price.

He has put King's in an excellent position to do so. Arthur Hearnden, General Secretary of the Independent Schools Joint Council, has observed that 'under Robin Reeve's leadership KCS has been one of the success stories of the past ten years. The School's steady rise to academic pre-eminence has made Westminster and St Paul's look to their laurels.' It is generally agreed among his colleagues that he has provided a clear sense of direction, of intellectual leadership and vision which has engendered confidence and pride in the School, not simply for its undoubted academic excellence, but as a civilised community. He would undoubtedly say that this has only been possible with the help of an able and enthusiastic Common Room. Among these have been distinguished heads of departments; Graham Tingay, Head of Classics until 1986, Eric Springthorpe, Head of Biology until 1990, Derek Pembery, Head of English until 1993, Stan Houston, Head of History since 1974, and in 1995 the longest-serving head of department, and Eddie Casale, Head of Mathematics until 1990, as well as an influential President of the Common Room.

Reeve's great achievement, in the opinion of Cavan Taylor, chairman of the Governing Body until 1990,

> has been to create throughout the School a climate of excellence. With his own exemplary academic record, it is not surprising that this side of the School's activities has gone from strength to strength. ... His intellectual rigour has been applied as much to the deliberations of the Building Committee, and Finance and General Purposes Committee of the Governing Body as it has to the structure and organisation of the academic side of the School. The public and private events of the

Opposite page: *South Hayes, rear view.*

School have been imbued, through Robin's influence, with great style and sense of occasion. But Robin is no arid martinet; his warmth, sensitivity and quiet sense of fun have also touched everything he has done in the School as, quite obviously, has his strong commitment to the Christian faith.

Sir Robert Andrew (KCS 1942–7), who became chairman of the Governing Body in 1990, considers that after the building programme of the 1980s and the recent property acquisitions the standard of the School's buildings is now generally good. Looking to the future he sees the need for one more major building project to cater for craft, design, and technology. He believes that the School was wise to wait until what was needed became more clear, but there is now a need to improve facilities for both art and technology and he hopes that a new building may be begun to mark the centenary in 1997 of the move to Wimbledon. More generally, he would like to see King's maintain its academic position in the first division of the country's schools, without becoming too preoccupied with examination league tables and while continuing to provide in a friendly atmosphere the balanced, all round education on which its reputation is based. On a personal note, as a former Surrey Scholar himself, he would welcome steps, against the background of the rising costs of independent schools, to make education offered at King's more readily available to boys from poorer backgrounds.

The purpose of King's as a school is the promotion of academic excellence, independence of mind, an enjoyment of learning, and realistic self-confidence. In addition it will surely continue to provide an ever more varied games programme and a stimulating range of school societies and activities. When Reeve retires in the School's centenary year at Wimbledon, he will have done all that one Head Master could do to make these worthy ambitions a reality.

Opposite page: *Head Master's assembly, Great Hall.*

Selected List of Old Boys

(*DNB*) indicates entry in *The Dictionary of National Biography*

THOMAS GOODWIN HATCHARD (1817–1870) Bishop of Mauritius. (*DNB*)

MAJOR-GENERAL SIR FREDERIC JOHN GOLDSMID (1818–1908) Responsible for the first transcontinental telegraph lines to India. (*DNB*)

STEPHEN PEARCE (1819–1904) Portrait and sporting artist. (*DNB*)

SIR MONIER MONIER-WILLIAMS (1819–1899) Oriental scholar. Founder of the Indian Institute, Oxford University. (*DNB*)

WILLIAM HIBBERT BINNEY (1819–1887) Bishop of Nova Scotia.

JONATHAN HOLT TITCOMB (1819–1862) First Bishop of Rangoon. (*DNB*)

JAMES JOHN BERKLEY (1819–1862) Railway engineer. Designed and built the first railway network in India. (*DNB*)

GEORGE DEVEY (1820–1886) Leading Victorian architect in the English vernacular style. (*DNB*)

SIR RICHARD ATWOOD GLASS (1820–1873) MP. Manufactured, laid, and operated the first successful Atlantic submarine cable. (*DNB*)

JOHN HENRY PEPPER (1821–1900) Professor of Chemistry, the Royal Polytechnic, Regent Street. Devised the stage illusion known as 'Pepper's Ghost'. (*DNB*)

SIR WALTER MORGAN (1821–1906) Chief Justice of Madras.

GEORGE FREDERICK POLLOCK (1821–1915) Senior Master of the Supreme Court and Queen's and King's Remembrancer.

HUMPHRY SANDWITH (1822–1881) Crimean War hero. Colonial Secretary to Mauritius. (*DNB*)

WILLIAM SHAKESPEARE BURTON (1824–1916) Artist in the Pre-Raphaelite style. His picture 'A Wounded Cavalier' was the sensation of the 1856 Royal Academy Exhibition.

JOHN WHICHCORD (1823–1885) Architect. PRIBA. (*DNB*)

JOHN COOPER FORSTER (1823–1886) Senior Surgeon, Guy's Hospital. PRCS. (*DNB*)

SIR EDWARD HERTSLET (1824–1902) Librarian and Keeper of Archives to the Foreign Office. (*DNB*)

SIR FRANCIS WYATT TRUSCOTT (1824–1895) Lord Mayor of London 1879.

ANDREW KENNEDY HUTCHINSON BOYD (1825–1899) Moderator of the General Assembly of the Church of Scotland. (*DNB*)

SAMUEL OSBORNE HABERSHON (1825–1889) Senior Physician, Guy's Hospital. President of the Medical Society of London. (*DNB*)

WILLIAM INCE (1825–1910) Professor of Divinity, Oxford University. (*DNB*)

WILLIAM BURGES (1827–1881) Victorian architect in the Gothic style. (*DNB*)

JACOB WREY MOULD (1825–1886) Chief Architect, New York City. Helped in the original design of Central Park.

ALFRED BARRY (1826–1910) Principal of Cheltenham College. Principal of King's College, London. Primate of Australia. (*DNB*)

LEONARD CHARLES WYON (1826–1891) Chief Engraver to the Royal Mint. (*DNB*)

JOHN SYER BRISTOWE (1827–1895) FRS. Neurologist. President of the Medical Society of London. (*DNB*)

WILLIAM THOMAS GORDON (1827–1900) Superior of the Brompton Oratory on six occasions.

SURGEON-GENERAL SIR WILLIAM GUYER HUNTER (1827–1902) MP. Surgeon-General of the Indian Army. (*DNB*)

GEORGE WILLIAM KITCHIN (1827–1912) Chancellor of Durham University. (*DNB*)

ROBERT HAYDON SHEBBEARE (1827–1860) Victoria Cross, the Indian Mutiny.

LIONEL SMITH BEALE (1828–1906) FRS. Professor of Medicine, London University. (*DNB*)

GEORGE BENTLEY (1828–1895) Editor. Publisher of many of the eminent Victorian writers. (*DNB*)

LEOPOLD DAVID LEWIS (1828–1890) Playwright. Translated *The Bells* from the French for Henry Irving. This was one of the latter's greatest successes. (*DNB*)

GEORGE JOSIAH PALMER (1828–1892) Founder/Editor of *The Church Times*. (*DNB*)

ROBERT TAYLOR PRITCHETT (1828–1907) Gun-maker to the British Government. Joint founder of the Working Men's College. Water colour painter to Queen Victoria. (*DNB*)

HENRY PARRY LIDDON (1829–1890) Dean Ireland's Professor, Oxford University. Canon of St Paul's Cathedral. (*DNB*)

CHARLES HENRY HOPWOOD (1829–1904) MP. Recorder of Liverpool. Founder of the Romilly Society. (*DNB*)

WILLIAM MICHAEL ROSSETTI (1829–1919) Original member of the Pre-Raphaelite Brotherhood. Literary critic and editor. (*DNB*)

DANTE GABRIEL ROSSETTI (1828–1882) Pre-Raphaelite poet and painter. (*DNB*)

WILLIAM AYERST (1830–1904) Founded the Ayerst Hostel in Cambridge. Elected to succeed Colenso as Bishop of Natal, but never consecrated owing to Church of England opposition. (*DNB*)

EDWARD MIDDLETON BARRY (1830–1880) RA. Professor of Architecture, the Royal Academy. (*DNB*)

SIR ALGERNON BORTHWICK, 1ST BARON GLENESK (1820–1908) MP. Proprietor and Editor of the *Morning Post*. (*DNB*)

FREDERICK GARD FLEAY (1830–1909) Polymath; literary critic; pioneer of spelling reform. (*DNB*)

SIR CHARLES HARBORD, 5TH BARON SUFFIELD (1830–1914) Courtier and intimate friend of Edward VII.

JOHN WHITAKER HULKE (1830–1895) FRS. Ophthalmologist. PRCS. (*DNB*)

PHILIP SALKELD (1830–1857) Victoria Cross, the Indian Mutiny.

ROBERT PATTEN ADAMS (1831–1911) Solicitor-General and Judge of the Supreme Court, Tasmania.

FREDERIC HARRISON (1831–1923) Positivist philosopher and literary critic. (*DNB*)

MARTIN HOWY IRVING (1831–1912) Professor of Classics and Vice-Chancellor, Melbourne University, Australia.

HENRY 'CAVENDISH' JONES (1831–1899) Joint founder of the All England Lawn Tennis Club, and its second Hon. Secretary. (*DNB*)

CHARLES BARON CLARKE (1832–1906) FRS. Botanist. Superintendent of the Botanical Gardens, Calcutta. (*DNB*)

THOMAS EDWIN BURTON BROWN (1833–1911) Master of the Apothecaries' Society.

HENRY FAWCETT (1833–1884) MP, FRS. Professor of Political Economy, Cambridge University. Postmaster-General. Established the parcel post 1883. (*DNB*)

SABINE BARING-GOULD (1834–1924) Copious author and writer of popular hymns, such as 'Onward, Christian Soldiers'. (*DNB*)

SIR ARTHUR HERBERT CHURCH (1834–1915) FRS. Discovered the animal pigment Turacin.

SIR WILLIAM HENRY PREECE (1834–1913) FRS. Pioneer of wireless telegraphy. Instituted the telephone system in England. (*DNB*)

WILLIAM GEORGE CUBITT (1835–1903) Victoria Cross, the Indian Mutiny. (*DNB*)

ALBERT VENN DICEY (1835–1922) Vinerian Professor of English Law, Oxford University. (*DNB*)

SIR WILLIAM GRANTHAM (1835–1911) MP. High Court Judge. (*DNB*)

CHRISTOPHER HEATH (1835–1905) Professor of Surgery, London University. PRCS. (*DNB*)

WALTER WILLIAM SKEAT (1835–1912) First Professor of Anglo-Saxon, Cambridge University. (*DNB*)

THOMAS ROSCOE REDE STEBBING (1835–1926) FRS. Zoologist.

EDWARD ARBER (1836–1912) Professor of English, Birmingham University. (*DNB*)

WORGAN JOHN FESTING (1837–1902) Bishop of St Albans. (*DNB*)

SIR SYDNEY GODOLPHIN ALEXANDER SHIPPARD (1837–1902) Judge of the Supreme Court, Cape Colony. (*DNB*)

SIR CHALONER ALABASTER (1838–1898) Consul-General, Canton

RICHARD PHENE SPIERS (1838–1916) Master of the Royal Academy Architectural School. President of the Architectural Association. (*DNB*)

LIONEL PERCY SMYTHE (1838–1918) RA. Landscape and genre painter.

ROLAND TRIMEN (1838–1916) FRS. Entomologist.

MAJOR-GENERAL EDWARD ROBERT FESTING (1839–1912) FRS. Director of the Science Museum.

INGRAM BYWATER (1840–1914) Regius Professor of Greek, Oxford University. (*DNB*)

SIR CHARLES DOUGLAS FOX (1840–1921) President of the Institute of Civil Engineers. (*DNB*)

EDMUND MOREL (1840–1871) Railway engineer. Built the first railway system in Japan in 1870.

CHARLES TAYLOR (1840–1908) Master of St John's College, Cambridge, and Vice-Chancellor of the University. (*DNB*)

THOMAS GIBSON BOWLES (1841–1922) MP. Journalist and founder of *Vanity Fair*. (*DNB*)

SIR EDWARD JAMES POLLOCK (1841–1928) Referee of the Supreme Court of Judicature.

SIR ALBERT KAYE ROLLIT (1842–1922) MP. President of the Incorporated Law Society.

SIR RICHARD EVERARD WEBSTER, 1ST VISCOUNT ALVERSTONE (1842–1915) MP. Lord Chief Justice, 1900–1913. (*DNB*)

MARK SEVER BELL (1843–1906) Victoria Cross, the Ashanti War.

SIR WILLIAM EMERSON (1843–1924) Pupil of William Burges. PRIBA.

SIR WILLIAM TURNER THISELTON-DYER (1843–1928) FRS. Director of Kew Gardens. (*DNB*)

SIR WILLIAM PURDIE TRELOAR (1843–1923) Lord Mayor of London 1906. Founded the Treloar Home for Crippled Children. (*DNB*)

HENRY TRIMEN (1843–1896) FRS. Director of the Botanical Gardens, Ceylon. (*DNB*)

SIR EDMUND WIDDRINGTON BYRNE (1844–1904) MP. High Court Judge. (*DNB*)

SIR ANDRIES STOCKENSTROM (1844–1880) Judge of the Supreme Court, Cape Colony.

SIR WILLIAM HENRY MAHONEY CHRISTIE (1845–1922) FRS. Astronomer-Royal. (*DNB*)

SIR JOHN BLUNDELL MAPLE (1845–1903) MP. Financier and philanthropist. (*DNB*)

LEOPOLD LIONEL ROTHSCHILD (1845–1917) Financier and sportsman.

GEORGE EDWARD BATEMAN SAINTSBURY (1845–1933) Professor of English, Edinburgh University. Oenophile. (*DNB*)

HENRY SWEET (1845–1912) Etymologist and Anglo-Saxon Scholar. (*DNB*)

CHARLES DELAUNEY TURNER, post BRAVO (1845–1876) Poisoned by antimony. The case was a *cause célèbre* in Victorian times and still remains unsolved.

EDWARD WAKEFIELD (1845–1924) Colonial Secretary, New Zealand Government.

CHARLES ALFRED ABSOLOM (1846–1889) Cambridge Blue, Kent and England cricketer. A member of the first MCC touring party to Australia in 1879, which initiated the Test Matches for the Ashes.

CHURCHILL JULIUS (1847–1938) Archbishop of Christchurch and Primate of New Zealand.

HENRY KEMBLE (1848–1907) Comic actor. (*DNB*)

JOHN MILNE (1850–1913) FRS. Seismologist. Professor at the Imperial University, Tokyo. (*DNB*)

SURGEON-GENERAL SIR GERALD BOMFORD (1851–1915) Director of the Indian Medical Service.

SIR JAMES GEORGE SCOTT (1851–1935) Burmese administrator. (*DNB*)

FREDERICK HENRY CHASE (1853–1925) President of Queens' College, Cambridge, and Vice-Chancellor of the University. Bishop of Ely. (*DNB*)

ERNEST JOHN BRUCE IWAN-MÜLLER (1853–1910) Leading journalist of his day. Friend and biographer of Lord Milner. (*DNB*)

JAMES GOW (1854–1923) Headmaster of Westminster School.

THOMAS ANSTEY GUTHRIE (1856–1934) Comic novelist and playwright under the name of F. Anstey. (*DNB*)

SIR SIDNEY JAMES MARK LOW (1857–1932) Historian and journalist. (*DNB*)

ALFRED WILLIAM POLLARD (1859–1944) Bibliographer and Shakespearian scholar. (*DNB*)

SIR JEREMIAH COLMAN (1860–1942) Financier and philanthropist, chairman of J. & J. Colman Ltd. A generous benefactor of KCS.

TERRICK JOHN WILLIAMS (1860–1936) RA. President of the Royal Institute of Painters in Water Colour.

JOSEPH CRAWHALL (1861–1913) Founder member of the Glasgow School of Artists, many of whose works are in the Burrell Collection.

BRIGADIER-GENERAL SIR JAMES EDWARD EDMONDS (1861–1956) Deputy Engineer-in-Chief, First World War. Took charge of the Official History of the First World War. (*DNB*)

WALTER RICHARD SICKERT (1860–1942) RA. The leading British Impressionist painter. (*DNB*)

ALFRED CHILTON PEARSON (1861–1936) Regius Professor of Greek, Cambridge University. (*DNB*)

ARTHUR BERESFORD PITE (1861–1934) Professor of Architecture, the Royal College of Art.

REGINALD MCKENNA (1863–1943) MP. First Lord of the Admiralty. Chancellor of the Exchequer. (*DNB*)

MAJOR-GENERAL SIR MAURICE PERCY CUE HOLT (1862–1954) Colonel Commandant of the RAMC.

SIR HERBERT JACKSON (1863–1936) FRS. Professor of Chemistry, London University. Pioneer in X-ray research. (*DNB*)

SIR JOHN MARTIN HARVEY (1863–1944) Actor-manager. (*DNB*)

FRANCIS ROBINSON PHELPS (1863–1938) Archbishop of Cape Town and Primate of South Africa.

HENRY HAVELOCK RAMSAY (1863–1929) Headmaster of Downside School. Abbot of Downside Abbey.

MAJOR-GENERAL SIR JOHN EMERSON WHARTON HEADLAM (1864–1946) Colonel Commandant of the RA.

SIR REGINALD WARD EDWARD LANE POOLE (1864–1941) President of the Law Society.

SIR THOMAS BELL (1865–1952) Marine engineer. Designed the turbines for HMS *Repulse* and *Hood* and for the *Queen Mary*. (*DNB*)

JAMES HARRY SEQUEIRA (1865–1948) The leading dermatologist of his day. (*DNB*)

THOMAS GREGOR BRODIE (1866–1916) FRS. Professor of Physiology, Toronto University, Canada.

ERNEST HENRY STARLING (1866–1927) FRS. Professor of Physiology, London University. (*DNB*)

JAMES LYNWOOD PALMER (1867–1941) Sporting artist. Carried out commissions for King George V.

SIR GEORGE ROWLAND BLADES, 1ST BARON EBBISHAM (1868–1953) MP. Lord Mayor of London, 1926.

SIR DANIEL EYERS GODFREY (1868–1939) Conductor and founder of the Bournemouth Symphony Orchestra.

WILLIAM WATSON (1868–1919) FRS. Professor of Physics, the Royal College of Science.

CALOUSTE SARKIS GULBENKIAN (1869–1955) Multimillionaire financier, philanthropist, and patron of the arts.

SIR LOUIS STUART (1870–1949) Chief Judge of Oudh Chief Court.

VERNON HERBERT BLACKMAN (1872–1967) FRS. Professor of Plant Physiology, London University. (*DNB*)

GEORGE HOLT THOMAS (1870–1929) Aviation pioneer. Founder of Imperial Airways and sponsor of Geoffrey de Havilland. (*DNB*)

ADMIRAL OF THE FLEET SIR FREDERICK LAURENCE FIELD (1871–1945) First Sea Lord 1930. (*DNB*)

STEWART RANKEN DOUGLAS (1871–1936) FRS. Bacteriologist.

SIR JOCELYN FIELD THORPE (1872–1940) FRS. Professor of Organic Chemistry, London University.

BURNETT HILLMAN STREETER (1874–1937) Provost of The Queen's College, Oxford. (*DNB*)

JOHN SIDNEY BLYTHE BARRYMORE (1882–1942) American stage and film actor.

SIR FRANCIS GRAEME TYRRELL (1876–1964) Chief Secretary, Ceylon.

SIR ERNEST ARTHUR BRIDGES (1880–1953) Master of the Royal Mail Lines.

WILLIAM NEILSON JONES (1883–1974) Professor of Botany, Bedford College, London University.

SIR WALTER THOMAS LAYTON, 1ST BARON LAYTON (1884–1966) Scholar, statesman, and editor. (*DNB*)

SIR EDWARD HENRY GERALD SHEPHERD (1886–1967) HM Minister to Iceland.

SIR HUGH IMBERT PERIAM HALLETT (1886–1967) High Court Judge.

SIR HENRY MONCK-MASON MOORE (1887–1964) Governor of Kenya and of Ceylon.

SIR VICTOR EWINGS NEGUS (1887–1974) Hunterian Professor, the Royal College of Surgeons.

SIR HENRY LINNINGTON MARTYN (1888–1947) Surgeon Apothecary to the Royal Household at Windsor.

MAJOR-GENERAL HENRY PORTER WOLSELEY HUTSON (1893–1992) Chairman of the British Trust for Ornithology.

FREDERICK SOWREY (1893–1968) The second fighter pilot to shoot down a Zeppelin at night in the First World War. Awarded the DSO.

CHARLES HOWARD GOULDEN MILLIS (1894–1984) Managing Director of Baring Brothers. Vice-Chairman of the BBC.

RICHARD–WALTHER DARRE (1895–1953) Germany's Minister of Food and Agriculture, 1933–1942.

HENRY DOUGLAS DICKINSON (1899–1969) Professor of Economics, Bristol University.

KENNETH HORNE (1900–1975) Popular playwright and writer of film scripts.

MICHAEL AMBROSE CARDEW (1901–1983) Master potter. The first and most eminent of Bernard Leach's pupils. (*DNB*)

SIR CYRIL WILSON BLACK (1902–1991) MP. Financier and philanthropist.

KENNETH GORDON MCNEIL (1902–1970) Deputy Chairman of Lloyd's of London.

GEOFFREY EMETT BLACKMAN (1903–1980) FRS. Professor of Rural Economy, Oxford University. (*DNB*)

GEORGE ERIC HOWARD FOXON (1904–1986) Professor of Biology, London University.

FRANCIS GEORGE HOLE (1904–1973) Managing Director of British Transport Hotels. Chairman of the KCS Governors, 1950–1973.

THITINANT NA RANONG (1906–) Thai Ambassador to Malaysia.

DAVID KIGHLEY BAXANDALL (1905–1993) Director of the National Galleries of Scotland.

LESLIE SPENCER HEARNSHAW (1907–) Professor of Psychology, Liverpool University.

HAROLD GEORGE NEWCOMBE LEE (1907–) Leading lawn tennis player. A member of the successful 1933 Davis Cup Team, the last year in which Great Britain won the contest.

ARTHUR STEWART KING SCARF (1913–1941) Squadron-Leader, RAF. Posthumous Victoria Cross, 1946, for gallantry in Malaya.

HAROLD WILLIAM RODGERS (1907–) Professor of Surgery, Queen's University, Belfast.

TORD ALVAR QUAN LIDELL (1908–1981) BBC announcer and news reader. (*DNB*)

GENERAL SIR ALAN JOLLY (1910–1977) Quartermaster-General, Colonel Commandant of RAC.

SIR RONALD HUGH OWEN (1910–1988) Chairman of the British Insurance Association.

SIR JOHN VIVIAN DACIE (1912–) FRS. Haematologist.

FRANCIS ROY PLOMLEY (1914–1985) Entertainer. Created BBC Radio D*esert Island Discs*. (*DNB*).

SIR RALPH VINCENT CUSACK (1916–1978) High Court Judge.

HAROLD GARNET CALLAN (1917–1994) FRS. Professor of Natural History, St Andrews University.

SIR VICTOR HENRY GOODHEW (1919–) MP. Vice-Chairman, Consolidated Defence Committee.

HENRY DAVID HALSEY (1919–) Lord Bishop of Carlisle.

DONALD ANDREW FRANK MOORE RUSSELL (1920–) Professor of Classical Literature, Oxford University.

JAMES KEITH O'NEILL ('JIMMY') EDWARDS (1920–1988) Comic actor. Best known on radio for his role in 'Take It From Here'.

SIR JAMES REGINALD ALFRED BOTTOMLEY (1920–) Ambassador to South Africa.

ERIC WILLY SIMON (1921–) Professor of Botany, Queen's University, Belfast.

SIR WILLIAM STANLEY PEART (1922–) FRS. Professor of Medicine, London University.

LEONARD THOMAS COTTON (1922–) Dean of King's College Hospital Medical School. Hunterian Professor, Royal College of Surgeons.

DUDLEY BRIAN SPALDING (1923–) FRS. Professor of Heat Transfer, London University.

SIR RICHARD BRIAN MEREDITH KING (1920–) Permanent Secretary, Ministry of Overseas Development.

JOHN CECIL CLOAKE (1924–1985) Ambassador to Bulgaria.

ALAN ELLIOTT GUILE (1924–) Professor of Engineering, Leeds University.

EDWIN DOUGLAS RAMSAY SHEARMAN (1924–) Professor of Engineering, Birmingham University.

AIR VICE-MARSHAL RHYS TUDOR BRACKLEY JONES (1925–) Dean of the RAF Medical Branch. Cade Professor, the Royal College of Surgeons.

RICHARD EDWARD PASCO (1926–) Actor.

DAVID JOHN EDWARD INGRAM (1927–) Vice-Chancellor Kent University.

SIR ROBERT JOHN ANDREW (1928–) Permanent Under-Secretary of State, Northern Ireland Office. Chairman of the KCS Governors, 1990– .

PETER GERALD MOORE (1928–) Principal of the London Business School. Vice-Chairman of the University Grants Committee.

WERNER PAUL WOLF (1930–) Professor of Engineering and Science, Yale University.

JOHN WOOD (1931–) Director of the Serious Fraud Office.

JOHN RICHARD HARRIS (1932–) Professor of Egyptology, Durham University.

DEREK OGSTON (1932–) Professor of Medicine and Vice-Principal, Aberdeen University.

DERRICK JOHN AMOORE (1935–1992) Editor of BBC Television News.

CAVAN TAYLOR (1935–) Solicitor. Chairman of the KCS Governors, 1973–1990.

JOHN DALBY HIGGINS (1934–)
Scholar and author on topics relating to
opera. Arts and Obituaries Editor, *The
Times*.

DAVID BARTLETT REES (1936–1993)
Novelist. Carnegie Medal 1978 for the
best children's book of the year, *The
Exeter Blitz*.

CHRISTOPHER JOHN WARD (1937–)
Editor of the *Daily Express* 1981–1983.

JOHN ARTHUR HUGH CURRY (1938–)
Chairman of the All England Lawn
Tennis Club.

SIR STUART NEIL MCKINNON (1938–)
High Court Judge.

DAVID FREDERICK HORROBIN (1939–)
Professor of Medicine, Montreal
University. Founder of the pharmaceut-
ical company, Scotia.

ROGER DEREK ROBINSON (1939–)
Professor of English, Victoria University,
Wellington, New Zealand.

NEIL ROBERT CHALMBERS (1942–)
Director of the Natural History Museum.

FRANK ROBERTSON HARTLEY (1942–)
Vice-Chancellor of Cranfield University.
Special Adviser to the Prime Minister on
defence systems.

BERNARD JONATHAN EVERETT (1943–)
Ambassador to Guatemala City.

PETER JOHN GOODHEW (1943–)
Professor of Science and Engineering,
Liverpool University.

ROBIN GREVILLE HOLLOWAY (1943–)
Musicologist and a leading contemporary
composer.

ROBERT JOHN AYLING (1946–)
Director of British Airways.

CONAL ROBERT GREGORY (1947–)
MP for York 1983–1992.

DAVID LEONARD NOKES (1948–)
Literary Scholar. Awarded the James Tait
Black Prize 1985 for a biography of
Swift.

WILLIAM ANTHONY ALLEN (1949–)
Head of the Foreign Exchange Division
of the Bank of England.

MARTIN ROGER GOLDMAN
(1949–1984) Author of scientific books
and prizewinning scientific programmes
for radio.

DAVID JOHN MCKITTERICK (1949–)
Scholar and bibliographer. Fellow and
Librarian, Trinity College, Cambridge.
Author of books on bibliographical
topics.

DAVID LAWRENCE SHAW (1950–) MP
for Dover 1987– .

SIMON CONWAY MORRIS (1951–)
FRS. Palaeontologist.

CLIVE WILLIAM ASLET (1955–)
Editor of *Country Life*.

GANESH SITTAMPALAM (1979–)
Awarded First Class Honours in
Mathematics at Surrey University at the
age of 13. Listed in the *Guinness Book of
Records* as the youngest graduate in the
UK.

Index

a friend of ours "scorching down the Strand."

A widower with 9 small children

The illustrations in the index are taken from a hand-made magazine called The Sneezer, *produced by boys at the School in 1885.*